Tea Celebrations

Tea Celebrations

SPECIAL OCCASIONS FOR AFTERNOON TEA

A publication of *TeaTime* Magazine

hm | books

Editor: Lorna Reeves
Creative Director/Photography: Mac Jamieson
Art Director: Karissa Brown
Assistant Editor: Anne-Harris Jones
Copy Editor: Nancy Ogburn
Editorial Assistant: Amy Hannum
Stylist: Lucy Wilson Herndon
Senior Photographer: Marcy Black Simpson
Photographers: William Dickey, Sarah Swihart, Kamin H. Williams
Test Kitchen Director: Janice Ritter
Test Kitchen Professionals: Janet Lambert, Loren Wood
Contributing Test Kitchen Professional: Chantel Lambeth
Senior Digital Imaging Specialist: Delisa McDaniel
Digital Imaging Specialist: Clark Densmore

hoffmanmedia

President: Phyllis Hoffman DePiano
Executive Vice President/COO: Eric W. Hoffman
Executive Vice President/CCO: Brian K. Hoffman
Executive Vice President/CFO: G. Marc Neas
Vice President/Manufacturing: Greg Baugh
Vice President/Editorial: Cindy Smith Cooper
Vice President/Consumer Marketing: Silvia Rider

First published in 2012 by Hoffman Media, LLC
Birmingham, Alabama
With offices at
1900 International Park Drive, Suite 50
Birmingham, Alabama 35243
hoffmanmedia.com

ISBN 978-0-9770069-2-2

Printed in Mexico

On the cover:
Fruit-Topped Coconut Cream Tartlets (page 67), Lemon Mini Cupcakes (page 67), and Hazelnut French Macarons (page 65)
Recipe development and food styling by Janet Lambert
Photography by Sarah Swihart
Photo styling by Lucy W. Herndon

contents

70

80 48

introduction

In a day and age when we seem to move at far too fast a pace, teatime invites us to slow down and savor some of the best things in life—relationships, food, and tea.

We cherish this long-held tradition not out of mere sentimentality and nostalgia but rather because it allows us to reconnect with friends and family in ways that are deeper, more personal, and certainly more memorable than quick electronic exchanges via text message, e-mail, and social networks, as convenient as those may be. Spending time around the tea table affords us moments to listen and share, not just to hear and talk. We notice the sparkle of joyful eyes and detect the sorrow in others. We encourage. We comfort. We laugh. And most of all, we celebrate the importance of relationships.

Tea Celebrations offers delightful tea menus for eight annual occasions that draw us to our tables. From New Year's Day to Christmas, the holiday afternoon teas depicted in these pages are filled with delicious recipes created by the talented professionals in *TeaTime*'s test kitchen. A few of the dishes are classics that have appeared in the magazine but are far too good to allow to fade from our memories and our palates. Most of the recipes in this book are new, however, inspired by these special events and served in beautiful settings that are sure to spark your own creativity, among them, a lovely and impressive birthday-party tea.

Although the food and décor are of great importance, we should remember that the quality of the tea served is as critical as the complementary flavors each selection adds to the meal. We trust that our expert tea pairings for the various courses of each menu will set your mind at ease as you host your next party. Because there are different ways to prepare each type of tea, we have provided steeping guidelines on page 91 to ensure a successful infusion.

Whatever the occasion, we hope you will find herein inspiration for hosting a beautiful and flavorful afternoon tea that will allow you and your guests to savor memorable moments together. Ultimately, those are the ingredients for the perfect tea celebration.

EGGNOG CHEESECAKES
(RECIPE ON PAGE 86)

New Year's DAY

MENU
Sweet Potato Scones with Molasses-Honey Butter
☕ *Dragon Pearl Jasmine Tea*

Texas Caviar & Goat Cheese Crostini
Ham Salad Tea Sandwich Stacker
Reuben Tartlets
☕ *Shui Xian Oolong Tea*

Chocolate Roulade
Triple Nut Tarts
Coconut-Pineapple White Chocolate Bars
☕ *Darjeeling Autumnal-Flush Black Tea*

pastry blender, cut butter into flour mixture until mixture resembles coarse crumbs. Set aside.

• In a small bowl, combine sweet potato puree, buttermilk, honey, and vanilla extract. Add milk mixture to flour mixture, stirring until just combined. (If mixture seems dry, add more buttermilk, 1 tablespoon at a time, until a dough forms.)

• Turn dough out onto a lightly floured surface, and knead lightly 5 times. Roll dough to a ½-inch thickness. Using a 3-inch cutter, cut as many scones as possible, rerolling scraps no more than twice. Place scones on prepared baking sheet.

• Bake until lightly browned, 15 to 20 minutes.

• Serve warm with Molasses-Honey Butter, if desired.

Preheat oven to 425°. Place 1 medium sweet potato on a foil-lined baking sheet. Bake until fork tender, approximately 45 minutes to 1 hour. Remove from oven, and let cool completely, approximately 1 hour. Peel potato and discard peel. Place potato pulp in the work bowl of a food processor. Puree until smooth.

Molasses-Honey Butter

Yield: 1¼ cups
Preparation: 10 minutes

1 cup butter, softened
3 tablespoons honey
1 tablespoon molasses

• In a small bowl, combine butter, honey, and molasses. Beat at medium speed with an electric mixer until smooth, approximately 2 minutes.

• Transfer mixture to a pastry bag fitted with a large star tip. Pipe mixture into desired butter pats. Refrigerate until needed.

Sweet Potato Scones

Yield: 8 to 10 scones
Preparation: 15 minutes
Bake: 15 to 20 minutes

1¾ cups all-purpose flour
2 tablespoons firmly packed light brown sugar
2½ teaspoons baking powder
1 teaspoon salt
½ teaspoon baking soda
6 tablespoons cold unsalted butter, diced
1 cup sweet potato puree*
⅓ cup buttermilk
2 tablespoons honey
1 teaspoon vanilla extract
1 recipe Molasses-Honey Butter (recipe follows)

• Preheat oven to 425°.

• Line a baking sheet with parchment paper. Set aside.

• In a large bowl, combine flour, brown sugar, baking powder, salt, and baking soda, whisking well. Using a

To serve accompanying butter or spreads, mix and match small dishes and dainty bowls, choosing the color and style that best fit the party's theme. Butter molds come in a variety of sizes and shapes and can add interesting touches to your tea table.

TEXAS CAVIAR AND
GOAT CHEESE CROSTINI
(RECIPE ON PAGE 12)

Texas Caviar & Goat Cheese Crostini

PHOTO
on page 11

Yield: 30 crostini
Preparation: 25 minutes
Refrigerate: 2 hours

2 (15.8-ounce) cans black-eyed peas, drained
1 (11-ounce) can whole-kernel corn, drained
⅓ cup minced yellow bell pepper
⅓ cup minced red bell pepper
⅓ cup minced green bell pepper
¼ cup chopped fresh cilantro
2 tablespoons chopped fresh parsley
¼ cup extra-virgin olive oil
¼ cup red-wine vinegar
1 teaspoon ground cumin
½ teaspoon kosher salt
½ teaspoon freshly ground black pepper
½ teaspoon garlic powder
1 (4-ounce) package goat cheese
30 slices toasted French baguette
Garnish: fresh chives

• In a medium bowl, combine peas, corn, bell peppers, cilantro, and parsley. Set aside.
• In a small bowl, combine olive oil, vinegar, cumin, salt, pepper, and garlic powder, whisking well. Pour over pea mixture, stirring to combine.
• Refrigerate for 2 hours. Drain, if necessary.
• Spread approximately ½ tablespoon goat cheese on each baguette slice, and top each with approximately 2 tablespoons pea mixture.
• Garnish with fresh chives, if desired. Serve immediately.

Ham Salad Tea Sandwich Stacker

Yield: 12 sandwiches
Preparation: 15 minutes

6 slices wheat bread
6 slices pumpernickel bread
6 slices white bread
¼ pound sliced deli ham, cut into 12 (2-inch) rounds
1 recipe Creamy Ham Salad (recipe follows)

1 recipe Watercress Pesto (recipe follows)
3 hard-boiled eggs, sliced
Garnish: fresh tarragon

• Using a 2-inch round cutter, cut 2 rounds from each bread slice. Discard scraps.
• Layer 1 wheat-bread round, 1 ham round, 1½ tablespoons Creamy Ham Salad, 1 pumpernickel-bread round, 1 tablespoon Watercress Pesto, 1 white-bread round, and 1 egg slice. Repeat with remaining ingredients.
• Secure stacks with wooden skewers.
• Garnish with fresh tarragon, if desired. Serve immediately.

Creamy Ham Salad

Yield: 2½ cups
Preparation: 10 minutes

1 (8-ounce) package cubed ham, drained
1 cup grated Gruyère cheese
1 (3-ounce) package cream cheese, softened
1 tablespoon coarse-grain mustard

• In the work bowl of a food processor, combine ham, cheeses, and mustard. Pulse until chunky. Refrigerate until needed.

NOTE: Store in an airtight container in the refrigerator for up to 5 days.

Watercress Pesto

Yield: 1 cup
Preparation: 5 minutes

¼ cup pecans, toasted
½ teaspoon minced garlic
2 cups loosely packed watercress
½ cup coarsely grated Parmesan cheese
¼ cup lemon-scented olive oil
¼ teaspoon salt

• In the work bowl of a food processor, combine pecans and garlic. Pulse until smooth. Add watercress, cheese, olive oil, and salt, pulsing until smooth. Use immediately.

"The tea party is a spa for the soul. You leave your cares and work behind. Busy people forget their business. Your stress melts away, your senses awaken."

—Alexandra Stoddard

Reuben Tartlets

Yield: 24 tartlets
Preparation: 10 minutes
Refrigerate: 2 hours
Bake: 15 minutes

1½ cups rye flour
1 cup cold unsalted butter, diced
½ cup sour cream
2 tablespoons caraway seeds
½ teaspoon kosher salt
¼ teaspoon freshly ground black pepper
1 recipe Mustard Sauce (recipe follows)
1 recipe Red Cabbage Slaw (recipe follows)
¼ pound thinly sliced deli corned beef, cut into
   1-inch strips
Garnish: baby lettuces

• In the work bowl of a food processor, combine flour, butter, sour cream, caraway seeds, salt, and pepper. Pulse until a dough forms.
• Remove dough, wrap in plastic wrap, and refrigerate for at least 2 hours.
• Preheat oven to 350°.
• On a lightly floured surface, roll dough to a ⅛-inch thickness. Using a 5-inch round cutter, cut 24 rounds from dough, rerolling scraps no more than once.
• Press rounds into bottoms and up sides of 24 (3-inch) brioche pans. Prick dough with a fork.
• Bake until lightly browned, approximately 15 minutes. Remove from oven, and let cool completely. Carefully remove tart shells from pans.
• Place approximately 1 teaspoon Mustard Sauce in the bottom of each tart shell. Top with approximately 2 tablespoons Red Cabbage Slaw. Layer 2 to 3 strips corned beef onto slaw.
• Garnish with baby lettuces, if desired. Serve immediately.

Mustard Sauce

Yield: approximately ¾ cup
Preparation: 5 minutes

½ cup mayonnaise
2 tablespoons Dijon-style mustard
1 tablespoon prepared horseradish
1 teaspoon chopped fresh tarragon
½ teaspoon kosher salt
¼ teaspoon freshly ground black pepper

• In a small bowl, combine mayonnaise, mustard, horseradish, tarragon, salt, and pepper, whisking well.

NOTE: Store in an airtight container in the refrigerator for up to 5 days.

Red Cabbage Slaw

Yield: approximately 3 cups
Preparation: 15 minutes
Cook: 30 minutes
Refrigerate: 2 hours

¼ cup butter
1 small red cabbage, thinly sliced
⅓ cup sherry vinegar
2 tablespoons sugar
1½ teaspoons salt

• In a large saucepan, melt butter over medium-high heat. Add cabbage, and cook, stirring often, until tender, approximately 10 minutes.
• Add vinegar, sugar, and salt. Reduce heat to medium-low, cover, and cook for 20 minutes.
• Let cool slightly. Refrigerate for 2 hours. Drain, if necessary.

NOTE: Store covered in an airtight container in the refrigerator for up to 3 days.

Chocolate Roulade

Yield: 10 to 12 servings
Preparation: 1 hour
Bake: 13 minutes

1 (4-ounce) bar bittersweet chocolate
9 large eggs, separated
1 cup sugar, divided
½ cup plus 3 tablespoons unsweetened natural cocoa
    powder, divided
1 tablespoon butter, melted
⅛ teaspoon salt
2 cups cold heavy whipping cream
½ cup plus 2 tablespoons confectioners' sugar, divided
1 teaspoon vanilla extract

• Preheat oven to 350°.
• Spray a rimmed 17-x-12-inch baking sheet with nonstick cooking spray. Line with parchment paper. Spray again. Set aside.
• Melt chocolate according to package directions. Let cool to room temperature. Set aside.
• In a mixing bowl, beat egg yolks at high speed with an electric mixer until light colored and slightly thick. Add ½ cup sugar, and beat until thick and pale yellow. Add melted chocolate, 3 tablespoons cocoa powder, butter, and salt, beating just until incorporated. Set aside.
• In a separate mixing bowl, beat egg whites at high speed until soft peaks form. Add remaining ½ cup sugar in a steady stream, and beat at high speed until stiff peaks form.
• Using a rubber spatula, vigorously fold half of egg whites into chocolate mixture. Gently fold remaining egg whites into mixture just until white streaks are gone.
• Pour mixture into prepared baking sheet, spreading until smooth and level.
• Bake until a wooden pick inserted in center comes out clean, approximately 13 minutes.
• While cake is baking, sprinkle a clean dish towel evenly with 2 tablespoons cocoa powder.
• When cake is done, immediately run a small sharp knife around edge of cake to loosen from pan. Sprinkle surface lightly with 2 tablespoons cocoa powder, and lay dish towel over cake, cocoa side down. Place a wire rack over towel, then invert cake onto towel.
• Remove parchment paper, and roll cake and towel together jelly-roll style. Let cool to room temperature.
• While cake is cooling, beat cream at high speed with an electric mixer until soft peaks form. Add ½ cup

confectioners' sugar and vanilla extract, beating until stiff peaks form. Add remaining ¼ cup cocoa powder, beating until incorporated.
• When cake is cool, gently unroll, and remove dish towel. Spread cake with whipped-cream mixture. Reroll cake jelly-roll style, seam side down.
• Serve immediately, or cover and refrigerate. When ready to serve, dust with remaining 2 tablespoons confectioners' sugar, and slice into serving pieces.

Triple Nut Tarts

Yield: 9 tarts
Preparation: 30 minutes
Refrigerate: 15 minutes
Bake: 13 to 15 minutes

½ (14.1-ounce) package refrigerated pie dough
    (1 sheet)
1 large egg
½ cup firmly packed brown sugar
3 tablespoons corn syrup
1 tablespoon butter, melted
1 teaspoon vanilla extract
1 teaspoon fresh orange zest
¼ cup chopped toasted, salted pistachios
¼ cup chopped toasted walnuts
¼ cup chopped toasted blanched almonds
Garnish: sugared orange curls

- Preheat oven to 350°.
- Unroll pie dough on a lightly floured surface. Using a 4-x-2¼-inch diamond-shaped tart pan, cut 9 shapes from dough. Press shapes into tart pans, trimming edges as necessary.
- Refrigerate for 15 minutes.
- In a medium bowl, combine egg, brown sugar, corn syrup, butter, vanilla extract, and orange zest, stirring until all ingredients are combined. Add nuts, stirring well.
- Divide mixture evenly among prepared tart pans.
- Bake until filling is set, approximately 13 to 15 minutes.
- Let cool to room temperature.
- Garnish each with a sugared orange curl, if desired.

Coconut-Pineapple White Chocolate Bars

Yield: 30 bars
Preparation: 1 hour
Refrigerate: 2 hours
Bake: 15 to 20 minutes
Cool: 20 minutes

½ cup unsalted butter, softened
¼ cup butter-flavored shortening
¼ cup plus 3 tablespoons sugar
2 teaspoons heavy whipping cream
½ teaspoon vanilla extract
¼ teaspoon salt
1¾ cups all-purpose flour
½ cup chopped dried pineapple
1 cup toasted sweetened flaked coconut, divided
10 (1-ounce) squares white baking chocolate, divided
¼ cup sweetened condensed milk
½ teaspoon coconut extract
8 ounces vanilla-flavored candy coating

- In a large bowl, combine butter and shortening. Beat at medium-high speed with an electric mixer for 1 minute.
- Add sugar, cream, vanilla extract, and salt, beating until combined. Add flour, pineapple, and ¼ cup coconut. Mix at low speed until combined.
- Divide into 2 portions. Wrap each portion in plastic wrap, and refrigerate for at least 2 hours.
- In a small saucepan, combine 7 squares white chocolate and condensed milk. Cook over low heat, whisking constantly until melted. Remove from heat. Add coconut extract, stirring to combine. Let cool slightly.

- Preheat oven to 350°.
- Line a rimmed baking sheet with parchment paper. Set aside.
- On a lightly floured surface, roll half of dough into a 10-x-8-inch rectangle approximately ¼ inch thick. Spread chocolate mixture over dough.
- Roll remaining dough into a 10-x-8-inch rectangle approximately ¼ inch thick. Place atop chocolate-covered dough, and gently press edges with fingers to seal. Transfer to prepared baking sheet.
- Bake until light golden brown, 15 to 20 minutes. Let cool completely.
- Transfer to a cutting board. Cut into 2¾-x-1¼-inch bars. Set aside.
- Place candy coating in a microwave-safe bowl. Heat coating in a microwave oven on High (100 percent power) in 30-second intervals until melted, stirring between each interval, approximately 1½ minutes total.
- Dip bottoms of bars into melted coating. Place bars coated side up on parchment paper to dry.
- Melt remaining 3 squares white chocolate in the same manner as candy coating.
- Spoon a strip of melted white chocolate across each bar. Sprinkle with remaining ¾ cup coconut. Let dry for at least 30 minutes.

NOTE: Store covered at room temperature for up to 5 days.

"There is no trouble so great or grave that cannot be much diminished by a nice cup of tea."

—Bernard-Paul Heroux

Valentine's DAY

MENU

Cherry-Almond Scone
🍵 *Vietnam Imperial Oolong Tea*

Artichoke Phyllo Cups
Roasted Pepper-Cheese Canapés
Sweet Currant & Cranberry Tea Sandwiches
🍵 *Darjeeling Pouchong Arya Green Tea*

Raspberry Heart French Macarons
Baked Cherry Heart Tartlets
Coconut-Pecan Palmier Hearts
🍵 *Chocolate Black Tea*

Cherry-Almond Scone

Yield: 12 scones
Preparation: 15 minutes
Bake: 20 minutes

2 cups self-rising soft wheat flour*
¼ cup sugar
½ cup cold heavy whipping cream
1 large egg
1 teaspoon almond extract
¼ cup cold salted butter
½ cup dried cherries
½ cup chopped blanched almonds, toasted
1 teaspoon caster sugar, optional

• Preheat oven to 350°.
• Line a baking sheet with parchment paper. Set aside.
• In a medium bowl, combine flour and sugar, whisking until combined. Set aside.
• In a small bowl, combine cream, egg, and almond extract, whisking well. Set aside.
• Using a pastry blender, cut butter into flour mixture until mixture resembles coarse crumbs. Add cherries and almonds, tossing to combine. Add cream mixture, stirring until a soft dough forms. (If mixture seems dry, add more cream, 1 tablespoon at a time, until a dough forms.)
• Using a levered 3-tablespoon scoop, drop scones onto prepared baking sheet. Sprinkle with caster sugar, if desired.
• Bake until edges are light golden brown, approximately 20 minutes.

For testing purposes, we used White Lily Enriched Bleached Self-Rising Flour, available in grocery stores throughout the Southeastern United States and online at whitelily.com.

Artichoke Phyllo Cups

Yield: 30 mini tarts
Preparation: 10 minutes
Bake: 10 minutes

1 cup quartered canned artichoke hearts
2 tablespoons mayonnaise
1 tablespoon sour cream
½ teaspoon fresh lemon zest
1 tablespoon fresh lemon juice
⅛ teaspoon ground black pepper
30 mini phyllo cups
Garnish: paprika and fresh lemon-zest curls

• Preheat oven to 350°.
• Blot artichoke hearts dry with a paper towel. Chop finely.
• In a small bowl, combine chopped artichokes, mayonnaise, sour cream, lemon zest, lemon juice, and pepper, stirring to combine. Divide mixture among phyllo cups. Place phyllo cups on a rimmed baking sheet.
• Bake until hot, approximately 10 minutes.
• Garnish with paprika and lemon-zest curls, if desired.
• Serve immediately.

Roasted Pepper-Cheese Canapés

Yield: 20 canapés
Preparation: 20 minutes

2 (5.2-ounce) packages garlic and herb Gournay cheese*, softened
2 tablespoons very finely minced roasted red pepper
5 slices firm whole wheat bread†
Garnish: roasted red pepper hearts‡

• In a small bowl, combine cheese and minced roasted red pepper, stirring to incorporate. Place in a piping bag fitted with a small open-star tip. Set aside.
• Using a round 1½-inch cutter, cut rounds from bread. Discard crusts.
• Pipe cheese in a decorative swirl onto each bread round.
• Garnish with a roasted red pepper heart, if desired.

For testing purposes, we used Boursin Garlic and Fine Herbs Gournay Cheese.

†*For testing purposes, we used Pepperidge Farm Farmhouse Style Whole Wheat Bread.*

‡*Using a very small heart cutter, cut small hearts from whole slices of roasted red pepper. Blot dry with a paper towel.*

"And although tea for one is certainly a fine thing, the addition of a circle of dear friends to share it with ensures the whole is larger than its parts."

—Author Unknown

HELPFUL
How-tos

For step-by-step
assembly photos,
turn to page 93.

Sweet Currant & Cranberry Tea Sandwiches

Yield: 18 sandwiches
Preparation: 15 minutes

1 (16-ounce) loaf sliced pumpernickel bread
2 (3-ounce) packages cream cheese, softened
2 tablespoons currant jelly
2 tablespoons cranberry chutney
1 tablespoon tea honey*

• Cut 36 (2¼-inch) squares from bread slices. Discard crusts.
• Using a 1-inch heart-shaped cutter, remove centers from half of bread squares. Set aside.
• In a small bowl, combine cream cheese, jelly, chutney, and honey, beating well. Spread approximately 1 tablespoon onto each bread square. Top each with a square with center removed. Serve immediately.

*For testing purposes, we used Savannah Bee Company Tea Honey, savannahbee.com.

Raspberry Heart French Macarons

Yield: approximately 24 sandwich cookies
Preparation: 40 minutes
Bake: 15 to 20 minutes
Cool: 30 minutes

3 large egg whites
4 drops red food coloring
2 tablespoons superfine sugar
1¾ cups confectioners' sugar
¾ cup slivered almonds
¼ cup dehydrated raspberries*, finely pulsed
1½ cups Buttercream Filling (recipe follows)

• Line 2 baking sheets with parchment paper. Set aside.
• In a mixing bowl, beat egg whites and food coloring at high speed with an electric mixer until frothy. Gradually add superfine sugar, beating until stiff glossy peaks form. Set aside.
• In the work bowl of a food processor, combine confectioners' sugar, almonds, and raspberries. Pulse until finely ground. Fold nut mixture into egg-white mixture.
• Spoon mixture into a pastry bag fitted with a large round tip. Pipe small V's (approximately 1 inch in diameter) onto prepared baking sheets. Let sit at room temperature for 30 minutes.

• Meanwhile, preheat oven to 275°.
• Bake until tops are set, hard, and dry but not cracked, 15 to 20 minutes. Let cool on baking sheets for 30 minutes.
• Spread Buttercream Filling on the bottom of a macaron. Sandwich with another macaron. Repeat with remaining macarons and Buttercream Filling.
• Store in an airtight container at room temperature for up to 1 week.

*For testing purposes, we used Just Raspberries, justtomatoes.com.

Buttercream Filling

Yield: 2½ cups
Preparation: 20 minutes

3 large egg whites
¾ cup sugar
1 cup unsalted butter, cut into tablespoons and softened
3 tablespoons cream cheese, cut into tablespoons and softened
1 teaspoon vanilla extract

• In the bowl of a stand mixer set over a pan of simmering water, combine egg whites and sugar. Whisk constantly until mixture registers 140° on an instant-read candy thermometer. Remove from heat.
• Place bowl on stand mixer, and beat mixture at high speed until egg whites are fluffy and cooled, approximately 10 minutes.
• Reduce mixer speed to medium-low. Add butter and cream cheese, by tablespoonfuls, mixing well after each addition. Add vanilla extract, mixing well. Use immediately.

- In a small bowl, combine egg yolk and water, whisking well to make an egg wash. Using a pastry brush, lightly coat a 1-inch border on half of dough hearts.
- Place approximately 1½ tablespoons cherry mixture in the centers of dough hearts brushed with egg wash. Top with remaining dough hearts. Using a fork, press gently to seal edges. Transfer to prepared baking sheet. Brush tops of hearts with remaining egg wash. Sprinkle with sanding sugar.
- Bake until golden brown, approximately 20 minutes. Remove from oven, and let cool for 10 minutes.
- Garnish serving platter with edible glitter, if desired.

*For testing purposes, we used Wilton Edible Heart Gold Glitter, wilton.com.

Baked Cherry Heart Tartlets

Yield: approximately 18 tartlets
Preparation: 20 minutes
Cook: 15 minutes
Bake: 20 minutes
Cool: 10 minutes

1 (10-ounce) package frozen cherries, thawed
¼ cup sugar
2 tablespoons cool water
1 tablespoon cornstarch
1 (14.1-ounce) package refrigerated pie dough (2 sheets)
1 large egg yolk
2 tablespoons water
2 tablespoons coarse sanding sugar
Garnish: edible glitter*

- In a small saucepan, combine cherries and sugar. Cook over medium heat, stirring often, until sugar is dissolved, approximately 10 minutes.
- Meanwhile, in a small bowl, combine water and cornstarch, whisking well. Add cornstarch mixture to cherry mixture. Bring to a boil, stirring constantly, and continue to cook until mixture thickens, 2 to 3 minutes. Remove from heat, and let cool completely.
- Preheat oven to 450°.
- Line a rimmed baking sheet with parchment paper. Set aside.
- Using a rolling pin, on a lightly floured surface, flatten dough slightly. Using a 4-inch heart-shaped cutter, cut as many hearts as possible from dough.

Coconut-Pecan Palmier Hearts

Yield: approximately 42 palmiers
Preparation: 10 minutes
Refrigerate: 1 hour
Bake: 8 to 10 minutes
Cool: 5 minutes

3 tablespoons sugar
3 tablespoons finely shredded sweetened coconut
2 tablespoons finely chopped pecans
1 tablespoon firmly packed light brown sugar
½ teaspoon salt
1 (17-ounce) package puff pastry dough

- Preheat oven to 400°.
- Line several baking sheets with parchment paper. Set aside.
- In a small bowl, combine sugar, coconut, pecans, light brown sugar, and salt, whisking well. Sprinkle approximately 2 tablespoons sugar mixture onto a work surface.
- Place half of pastry dough on prepared surface. Sprinkle with approximately 2 tablespoons sugar mixture. Using a rolling pin, roll dough into a 10-inch square.
- Fold in 2½ inches of opposite sides of dough square. Repeat.
- Fold half of dough over the other lengthwise. Cut crosswise into 1-inch slices. Dip cut side of slices into sugar mixture. Place pastries cut side down approximately 2 inches apart on prepared baking sheets, pinching bottom fold. Repeat with remaining dough and remaining sugar mixture, baking in batches.
- Bake until golden brown, 8 to 10 minutes. Let cool on baking sheet for 5 minutes. Transfer to wire racks to cool completely.

HELPFUL
How-tos

For step-by-step
assembly photos,
turn to page 92.

St. Patrick's DAY

MENU

Irish Soda Scones
☕ *Irish Breakfast Black Tea*

Potato-Leek Soup
Irish Lamb & Barley Stew in Patty Shells
Corned Beef Tea Sandwiches with Mustard Butter
☕ *Gunpowder Green Tea*

Lemon-Mint Cheesecake Bars
Chocolate-Guinness Mini Cupcakes
Green Grape & Pistachio Cream Pavlovas
☕ *Creamy Earl Grey Black Tea*

- Using a levered 3-tablespoon scoop, drop dough onto prepared baking sheet.
- Bake until edges are light golden brown and a wooden pick inserted in centers comes out clean, approximately 15 minutes.
- Serve with lingonberry jam and clotted cream, if desired.

Lingonberries are related to cranberries. Lingonberry jam can be found at specialty-foods stores and online. Substitute a favorite jam, if desired.

Potato-Leek Soup

Yield: 2 quarts
Preparation: 30 minutes
Cook: 30 minutes

3 tablespoons butter
2 cups sliced leeks, white part only (¼-inch slices)
1 quart chicken broth
1 cup water
8 cups cubed peeled potato*
2 teaspoons salt
1 cup heavy whipping cream
Garnish: microgreens

- In a large nonstick saucepan, melt butter over medium-high heat. Add leeks, stirring and cooking until leeks start to turn light brown around the edges, 2 to 3 minutes. Reduce heat to low.
- Cook, covered, stirring occasionally until leeks are caramelized, soft, and tender, approximately 10 minutes.
- Add chicken broth, water, potatoes, and salt. Bring to a boil. Reduce heat to low, and cover.
- Simmer, stirring occasionally, until potatoes are very tender when pierced with a fork, approximately 20 minutes.
- Remove from heat, and add cream.
- Using a hand-held immersion blender, puree until very creamy and smooth.[†]
- Serve warm.
- Garnish with microgreens, if desired.

For testing purposes, we used russet potatoes. For correct consistency and taste, it is important to use a starchy potato.

[†]Alternatively, pour mixture into the container of a regular blender, and puree until creamy and smooth.

Irish Soda Scones

Yield: 8 to 11 scones
Preparation: 10 minutes
Bake: 15 minutes

2 cups bread flour
2 tablespoons sugar
1 teaspoon baking soda
½ teaspoon salt
¼ cup cold salted butter
¼ cup dried currants
1 teaspoon caraway seeds
¾ cup plus 2 tablespoons whole buttermilk
Lingonberry jam* (optional)
Clotted cream (optional)

- Preheat oven to 350°.
- Line a baking sheet with parchment paper. Set aside.
- In a medium bowl, combine flour, sugar, baking soda, and salt, whisking until combined. Using a pastry blender, cut butter into flour mixture until mixture resembles coarse crumbs. Add currants and caraway seeds, stirring to combine. Add buttermilk, stirring until a soft dough forms. (If mixture seems dry, add more buttermilk, 1 tablespoon at a time, until dough is uniformly moist.)

HELPFUL *Hint*

Vintage green glass bowls add color and personality to the tea table. Look for them at antiques stores, estate sales, and online at *replacements.com*.

- Bake pastry shells according to package directions.
- Fill pastry shells with warm lamb stew.
- Garnish each serving with a fresh thyme sprig, if desired.
- Serve immediately.

For testing purposes, we used Pepperidge Farm Puff Pastry Shells.

†*At this point, mixture can be covered and stored in the refrigerator for a day. When ready to serve, heat to boiling, and then reduce heat to low. Thicken with cornstarch mixture.*

Irish Lamb & Barley Stew in Patty Shells

Yield: 8 servings
Preparation: 20 minutes
Cook: 20 to 23 minutes

2 tablespoons butter
1 teaspoon olive oil
¼ cup minced onion
¼ cup minced celery
¼ cup finely diced carrot
½ pound ground lamb
¼ teaspoon garlic salt
⅛ teaspoon ground black pepper
2 cups chicken broth
1 teaspoon fresh thyme leaves
½ cup cooked pearl barley
3 tablespoons Marsala cooking wine
1 teaspoon cornstarch
1 tablespoon water
8 frozen puff pastry shells*
Garnish: fresh thyme sprigs

- In a medium nonstick sauté pan, heat butter over medium-high heat until butter melts. Add olive oil. Add onion, celery, carrots, lamb, garlic salt, and pepper to pan. Cook, stirring frequently, until lamb is browned and vegetables are tender, 3 to 5 minutes.
- Add broth, thyme, and barley. Bring to a boil. Reduce heat to low, cover, and cook for 15 minutes, stirring occasionally. Add Marsala.†
- In a small bowl, combine cornstarch and water, stirring until smooth. Add to lamb stew, stirring and cooking until mixture is thickened and broth is clear, 2 to 3 minutes.

Corned Beef Tea Sandwiches with Mustard Butter

Yield: 16 tea sandwiches
Preparation: 15 minutes

½ cup butter, softened
2 tablespoons spicy brown mustard
2 teaspoons dill pickle relish
6 slices oatmeal bread*
16 thin slices deli top round corned beef
Garnish: sliced cornichons

- In a small bowl, combine butter, mustard, and relish, stirring well.
- Spread butter mixture onto 1 side of each bread slice.
- Place 4 slices corned beef in a ruffled pattern on buttered side of 2 bread slices. Top each with a buttered bread slice, buttered side down. Spread each bread slice with more butter mixture. Top each with another 4 slices corned beef in a ruffled pattern. Top each with a remaining bread slice, buttered side down.†
- Using a sharp, serrated knife, cut crusts from sandwich. Cut each sandwich in half and then each half into 4 square pieces.
- Garnish each sandwich with a cornichon slice, and secure with a green-frilled toothpick, if desired.

For testing purposes, we used Pepperidge Farm Farmhouse Style Oatmeal Bread.

†*Sandwiches may be made early in the day, left whole, draped with a slightly dampened paper towel, and kept in a covered container in the refrigerator. Slice into individual sandwiches just before serving.*

Lemon-Mint Cheesecake Bars

Yield: 36 bars
Preparation: 30 minutes
Cook: 5 minutes
Bake: 38 minutes
Cool: 1 hour
Refrigerate: 4 hours

1¼ cups graham-cracker crumbs
½ cup plus 3 tablespoons sugar, divided
⅓ cup butter, melted
2 (8-ounce) packages cream cheese, softened
2 large eggs
1 tablespoon fresh lemon zest
⅓ cup fresh lemon juice
½ cup mint jelly

• Preheat oven to 325°.
• Line a 9-inch square baking pan with foil and parchment combination paper with parchment side facing up, hanging over sides of pan to create handles to lift cheesecake. Set aside.
• In a medium bowl, combine graham-cracker crumbs, 3 tablespoons sugar, and melted butter, stirring until combined. Press into bottom of pan, creating a level surface.
• Bake until crust is lightly browned and firm to the touch, approximately 8 minutes. Let cool completely.
• In another medium bowl, beat cream cheese at high speed with an electric mixer until soft, creamy, and smooth. Add eggs, lemon zest, lemon juice, and remaining ½ cup sugar, beating until incorporated into cream cheese.
• Spread mixture evenly over crust in prepared pan.

- In a small saucepan over low heat, melt mint jelly, whisking until completely smooth. Cool slightly, and then drop over cheesecake surface in 5 straight lines. Drag a chopstick, drinking straw, or knife through each line in a zigzag motion to form a pleasing swirled pattern.
- Bake until cheesecake is set and puffed, approximately 30 minutes. (A slight jiggle in the center is normal. Cheesecake will continue to cook and set after it is removed from oven.)
- Let cool completely on a wire rack. Cover, and refrigerate for at least 4 hours.
- Using foil overhang as handles, lift cheesecake from pan.
- Using a long, sharp knife, cut cheesecake into 36 square bars.

NOTE: *Mint jelly swirls may settle when cheesecake cools. If settling results in unsightly gaps, melt ¼ cup jelly, place in a piping bag fitted with a small tip or in a ziplock bag with the corner snipped off, and fill gaps in green swirl, if desired. Refrigerate for 1 hour to reset swirled pattern.*

Chocolate-Guinness Mini Cupcakes

Yield: 24 mini cupcakes
Preparation: 20 minutes
Cook: 5 minutes
Bake: 10 minutes

½ cup Guinness beer
¼ cup salted butter
1 cup plus 1 tablespoon sugar
1 large egg
⅓ cup sour cream
2 teaspoons vanilla extract
1 cup plus 1 tablespoon all-purpose flour
⅓ cup natural unsweetened cocoa powder
¾ teaspoon baking soda
¼ teaspoon salt
1 recipe Chocolate Buttercream Frosting (recipe follows)
Garnish: green cake sprinkles*

- Preheat oven to 350°.
- Spray a 24-well mini muffin pan† with nonstick cooking spray with flour. Set aside.
- In a medium saucepan, combine beer and butter over low heat, stirring just until butter melts. Remove from heat. Add sugar, stirring well. Set aside.

- In a small bowl, combine egg, sour cream, and vanilla extract, stirring just until blended. Add to beer mixture, stirring to incorporate. Set aside.
- In another small bowl, combine flour, cocoa, baking soda, and salt, whisking well. Add flour mixture to liquid mixture, stirring just until incorporated and fairly smooth. (Some lumps may remain.) Fill wells of prepared muffin pan three-fourths full.
- Bake until a wooden pick inserted in centers comes out clean, 10 to 11 minutes.
- Immediately remove cupcakes from pan. Let cool completely on wire racks.
- Place Chocolate Buttercream Frosting in a piping bag fitted with a large open-star tip, and pipe decorative swirls onto tops of cupcakes.
- Garnish with cake sprinkles, if desired.
- Store cupcakes covered in the refrigerator for up to 2 days.

For testing purposes, we used Wilton Green Cake Sparkles, wilton.com.

†*We used a Calphalon 24-well mini muffin pan. Wells have a 3-tablespoon capacity, which is a bit more than that of other brands. Using another brand may result in leftover batter.*

Chocolate Buttercream Frosting

Yield: 2½ cups
Preparation: 5 minutes

1 cup salted butter, softened
3½ cups confectioners' sugar
¼ cup natural unsweetened cocoa powder
¼ teaspoon salt
1½ teaspoons vanilla extract
3 tablespoons whole milk

- In a medium bowl, combine butter, confectioners' sugar, cocoa, salt, vanilla extract, and milk. Beat at low speed with an electric mixer. Increase power to high speed, beating until all ingredients are incorporated and mixture is smooth and fluffy, 2 to 3 minutes, and scraping down sides of bowl while beating if necessary. Use immediately, or cover and store in refrigerator. Let come to room temperature before using.

Green Grape & Pistachio Cream Pavlovas

Yield: 10 pavlovas
Preparation: 30 minutes
Bake: 1 hour
Cool: 2 hours

2 large egg whites, at room temperature
¼ teaspoon cream of tartar
¼ teaspoon lemon extract
⅛ teaspoon salt
½ cup sugar
1 (3-ounce) box instant pistachio pudding mix
1½ cups cold whole milk

2 tablespoons sour cream
2 cups green grapes, halved lengthwise
2 tablespoons finely chopped pistachios
Garnish: fresh mint

• Preheat oven to 250°.
• Line a baking sheet with parchment paper. Using a 2-inch round cutter and a pencil, trace 10 circles, 2 inches apart, onto parchment. Flip parchment over so pencil marks are face down on baking sheet. Set aside.
• In a medium bowl, combine egg whites, cream of tartar, lemon extract, and salt. Beat at high speed with an electric mixer until soft peaks form. Add sugar gradually while beating until stiff peaks form. (Meringue mixture will look glossy.)
• Place mixture in a piping bag fitted with a medium (Wilton #21) open-star tip. Starting in the middle of each traced circle, pipe concentric circles outward until circle is filled. Pipe 1 to 2 extra layers on perimeters of rounds to form a rim around the edge.
• Bake for 1 hour. Turn off oven, and let sit in oven for at least 2 hours or overnight. (This will help meringues continue to dry and form a crispy shell.)
• In another medium bowl, combine pudding mix and cold milk, whisking constantly until mixture thickens, 2 to 3 minutes. Add sour cream, stirring to blend. Cover, and refrigerate until ready to use.
• Divide pistachio cream evenly among meringue shells. Arrange grape halves in concentric layers in pistachio cream to form a flower shape. Sprinkle chopped pistachios over pistachio cream.
• Garnish with mint, if desired.
• Serve immediately.

By baking these pretty piped meringue shells at a low temperature for a long time, the moisture gradually dries out, leaving behind a sweet crisp base for filling. Here, each shell, or pavlova, holds creamy pistachio pudding and flavorful green grapes, creating a dessert that is visually impressive yet extraordinarily simple to make.

HELPFUL *How-tos*

For step-by-step photos, turn to page 93.

Easter

MENU

Coconut Scones
🍵 *Tropical Green Tea*

Carrot Fritters
Ham Salad Sandwiches
Mini Lamb Quiches with Parmesan Crisps
🍵 *Darjeeling Ambootia Estate Black Tea*

Lemon-Ginger Mini Tartlets
Crêpes & Blueberry Sauce
Chocolate-Almond Surprise Coconut Cakes
🍵 *Wildberry Black Tea*

"Through the timeless ritual of savoring and sharing, tea adds depth and loveliness to every occasion."

—Susan Rios

Coconut Scones

Yield: 12 scones
Preparation: 20 minutes
Bake: 12 to 16 minutes

2 cups all-purpose flour
½ cup finely ground sweetened, shredded coconut, toasted
¼ cup sugar
1½ teaspoons baking powder
½ teaspoon finely grated fresh lemon zest
¼ teaspoon coarse salt
6 tablespoons shortening, chilled and cut into pieces
⅓ cup plus 2 tablespoons coconut milk, divided
1 tablespoon heavy whipping cream
½ teaspoon vanilla extract
Prepared lemon curd (optional)

• Preheat oven to 400°.
• Line a baking sheet with parchment paper. Set aside.
• In a medium bowl, combine flour, coconut, sugar, baking powder, lemon zest, and salt, whisking to combine. Using a pastry blender, cut shortening into flour mixture until mixture resembles coarse crumbs.
• Add ⅓ cup coconut milk, cream, and vanilla extract, stirring with a wooden spoon until all ingredients are combined and a soft dough forms. (If dough seems dry, add more cream, 1 tablespoon at a time, until a dough forms.)
• On a lightly floured surface, roll dough to ½-inch thickness. Using a 2-inch square cutter, cut 12 scones, rerolling scraps only once. Place scones 2 inches apart on prepared baking sheet.
• Brush tops of scones with remaining 2 tablespoons coconut milk.
• Bake until bottom edges are light golden brown, 12 to 16 minutes. Transfer to wire racks to cool slightly.
• Serve with lemon curd, if desired.

Carrot Fritters

PHOTO
on page 38

Yield: 12 fritters
Preparation: 30 minutes
Bake: 18 to 22 minutes

¾ cup plain yogurt
½ cup minced fresh chives
¼ cup sour cream
3 tablespoons minced fresh parsley
1 teaspoon finely grated fresh lemon zest
1 tablespoon fresh lemon juice
1 pound carrots, peeled and shredded
1½ cups panko-style bread crumbs
3 large eggs
1 cup chopped green onion
1 teaspoon coarse salt
½ teaspoon ground black pepper
¼ teaspoon ground nutmeg
12 seeded round crackers* (optional)
Garnish: finely chopped toasted walnuts

• Preheat oven to 350°.
• Line a baking sheet with parchment paper. Set aside.
• In a small bowl, combine yogurt, chives, sour cream, parsley, lemon zest, and lemon juice. Stir until mixture is well combined. Cover, and refrigerate for at least 30 minutes.
• In a large bowl, combine carrots, bread crumbs, eggs, green onion, salt, pepper, and nutmeg. Stir with a wooden spoon until mixture comes together.
• Place a 3½-inch round biscuit cutter on prepared baking sheet. Fill each biscuit cutter three-fourths full, lightly pressing down to release any air bubbles. Carefully slide cutter up and away from carrot filling. Repeat process with remaining carrot mixture.
• Bake until edges are golden brown, 18 to 22 minutes.
• Place each fritter atop a cracker, if desired. Transfer to a serving platter.
• Top each fritter with yogurt mixture.
• Garnish with toasted walnuts, if desired. Serve immediately.

For testing purposes, we used Carr's Table Water Crackers.

Mini Lamb Quiches with Parmesan Crisps

Yield: 12 mini quiches
Preparation: 30 minutes
Refrigerate: 1½ hours
Bake: 22 minutes

1 cup all-purpose flour
½ cup finely grated Parmesan cheese, divided
1 tablespoon sugar
¾ teaspoon coarse salt, divided
¾ teaspoon ground black pepper, divided
3 tablespoons shortening
5 tablespoons heavy whipping cream, divided
4 ounces ground lamb
⅓ cup finely chopped red onion
½ teaspoon minced garlic
3 tablespoons chopped roasted red bell pepper
2 tablespoons minced fresh basil
1 large egg, lightly beaten
1 recipe Parmesan Crisps (recipe follows)

• In the work bowl of a food processor, fitted with a metal blade, combine flour, ¼ cup Parmesan cheese, sugar, ¼ teaspoon salt, ¼ teaspoon black pepper, and shortening. Pulse until mixture is crumbly. Add 3 tablespoons cream, and pulse just until dough forms a ball. Wrap tightly in plastic wrap. Refrigerate until firm, approximately 1 hour.
• On a lightly floured surface, roll dough to a ⅛-inch thickness. Using a 4-inch square cutter, cut 12 squares, rerolling dough once if necessary. Fit a dough square into each well of a 12-well square tart pan with removable bottoms*. Firmly press into the bottom and up the sides of each well. Refrigerate for 30 minutes.
• Preheat oven to 350°.
• Prick bottom and sides of dough.
• Bake until edges are lightly golden, 8 to 10 minutes. Let cool.
• In a medium skillet, combine ground lamb, onion, and garlic. Cook over medium-high heat until lamb is browned and crumbly. Transfer mixture to a medium bowl, and let cool for 8 minutes.
• Add remaining ¼ cup Parmesan cheese, roasted bell pepper, remaining 2 tablespoons cream, basil, egg, remaining ½ teaspoon salt, and remaining ½ teaspoon pepper. Stir until mixture is well combined. Divide mixture evenly among tart shells.
• Bake until centers are set, 8 to 12 minutes.

Ham Salad Sandwiches

Yield: 24 tea sandwiches
Preparation: 20 minutes

½ pound thinly sliced deli Virginia ham
3 tablespoons minced black olives
3 tablespoons mayonnaise
1 tablespoon minced fresh parsley
2 teaspoons Dijon-style mustard
12 very thin slices sandwich bread
24 thin slices cucumber
Garnish: parsley leaves

• In the work bowl of a food processor fitted with a metal blade, combine ham, olives, mayonnaise, minced parsley, and mustard. Pulse until mixture is well combined but still has texture. Set aside.
• Using a 2- to 2½-inch tulip-shaped cutter*, cut 2 tulip shapes from each bread slice. Discard scraps.
• Place cucumber slices on serving platter. Top each slice with 1 tablespoon ham salad mixture. Top each with a bread tulip.
• Garnish with parsley leaves, if desired.

Tulip-shaped cutters can be found at wilton.com.

HELPFUL *Hint*

For a crunchy cheese bite, serve Parmesan Crisps in place of crackers with salads or soups.

• Remove from oven, and let cool slightly. Remove quiches from pan, and serve warm.
• Garnish with Parmesan Crisps, if desired.

For testing purposes, we used Chicago Metallic Lift & Serve Single Squares Pan.

Parmesan Crisps

Yield: 12 crisps
Preparation: 15 minutes
Bake: 8 minutes

¾ cup finely grated Parmesan cheese, divided
12 parsley leaves, divided

• Line a baking sheet with a silicone baking mat.
• Sprinkle 1 heaping tablespoon Parmesan cheese, forming a 2-inch round, on prepared baking sheet. Place a parsley leaf in the center. Repeat with remaining cheese and parsley, leaving 1 inch between rounds.
• Bake until lightly browned, approximately 8 minutes.
• Using a spatula, quickly remove cheese crisps from baking sheet. Let cool on a wire rack. Store at room temperature in an airtight container.

Lacy Parmesan Crisps inserted into warm Mini Lamb Quiches add height and decorative flair.

• In a small bowl, combine egg yolks and ¼ cup hot lemon mixture, whisking well. Add another ¼ cup hot lemon mixture, whisking constantly. (This will temper the eggs and prevent curdling). Add all of egg mixture back to pan with lemon mixture. Bring just to a boil, stirring constantly.
• Remove from heat, and add crystallized ginger, stirring well.
• Distribute lemon curd evenly among tartlet shells. Set aside.
• In a medium bowl, beat egg whites at high speed with an electric mixer until foamy. Gradually add remaining 2 tablespoons sugar, increasing speed to high and beating until stiff peaks form.
• Spoon meringue over filling in tartlet shells.
• Bake just until meringue browns, 7 to 8 minutes.
• Serve immediately, or refrigerate until ready to serve. (Tartlets are best made the day they will be eaten but can be made early in the day and refrigerated until ready to eat.)

For testing purposes, we used Clearbrook Farms Sweet Tart Shells.

Lemon-Ginger Mini Tartlets

Yield: 24 mini tartlets
Preparation: 30 minutes
Bake: 5 minutes

24 sweet tartlet shells*
½ cup plus 2 tablespoons sugar, divided
1 tablespoon all-purpose flour
1 tablespoon cornstarch
¼ teaspoon salt
¾ cup water
3 tablespoons fresh lemon juice
1 tablespoon fresh lemon zest
1 tablespoon butter
2 large eggs, yolks and whites separated
1 tablespoon finely minced crystallized ginger

• Preheat oven to 350°.
• Arrange tartlet shells on a rimmed baking sheet. Set aside.
• In a medium saucepan, combine ½ cup sugar, flour, cornstarch, and salt, whisking well. Add water, lemon juice, and lemon zest, whisking until combined. Cook over medium-high heat until mixture comes to a boil and thickens, stirring constantly. Remove from heat, and add butter, stirring well.

Crêpes & Blueberry Sauce

Yield: 24 crêpes
Preparation: 10 minutes
Cook: 20 minutes
Refrigerate: 2 hours

2 dry pints fresh blueberries
½ cup sugar, divided
2 tablespoons orange juice
1 cup cottage cheese
2¼ cups all-purpose flour
¼ teaspoon coarse salt
2 cups whole milk
3 large eggs, lightly beaten
1 tablespoon Grand Marnier liqueur
1 teaspoon vanilla extract
1½ tablespoons unsalted butter, melted
1 tablespoon vegetable oil

• In a medium saucepan, combine blueberries, ¼ cup sugar, and orange juice. Cook over medium heat until sugar dissolves. Bring to a rolling boil, stirring constantly, until mixture coats the back of a spoon and is thickened. Let mixture cool slightly before transferring to an airtight container to keep warm until needed.*

• In a small bowl, combine cottage cheese and 3 table-spoons sugar. Cover, and refrigerate until ready to use.

• In a large bowl, combine flour, remaining 1 table-spoon sugar, and salt. Add milk, eggs, Grand Marnier, and vanilla extract, whisking until well combined. Add melted butter and oil, whisking until mixture is smooth. Strain mixture through a fine-mesh strainer. Cover, and let batter stand for 2 hours, either in the refrigerator or at room temperature.†

• Heat a small skillet coated with nonstick cooking spray over medium-high heat. Remove pan from heat.

• Place a 3-inch round cookie cutter in hot pan. Pour approximately 1½ tablespoons batter into cutter. Quickly tilt pan in all directions, holding down the cutter so batter covers inside of cutter with a thin film. Cook for 20 to 30 seconds. Carefully remove cutter, and lift edge of crêpe with spatula to test for done-ness. Turn crêpe when underside is lightly browned.

Cook for 20 to 30 seconds on other side. Place crêpe on paper towel to cool.

• Repeat cooking procedure to make 24 crêpes, stacking crêpes between single layers of waxed paper to prevent sticking.

• Fill prepared crêpes with approximately 1 heaping table-spoon cottage cheese mixture. Fold 1 side over the other.

• Place 2 filled crêpes on each plate. Spoon warm blueberry sauce over crêpes. Serve immediately.

*Sauce can be made ahead, stored in the refrigerator, and warmed before serving.

†Store in an airtight container in the refrigerator for up to 3 days.

NOTE: Leftover batter can be stored in an airtight container in the refrigerator for up to 4 days.

Chocolate-Almond Surprise Coconut Cakes

Yield: 12 miniature cakes
Preparation: 30 minutes
Bake: 11 to 12 minutes
Cool: 30 minutes
Freeze: 1 hour

1 (16.5-ounce) box white cake mix*
3 large eggs
1 cup water
¼ cup canola oil
¼ cup sour cream
½ teaspoon vanilla extract
2 cups sweetened shredded coconut
1 recipe Dark Chocolate Filling (recipe follows)
¼ cup whole toasted almonds
1 recipe Fluffy Vanilla Frosting (recipe follows)
Garnish: sugared edible flowers†

• Preheat oven to 350°.
• Spray a 17-x-11½-inch rimmed baking sheet with nonstick cooking spray with flour. Line with parchment paper, and spray again. Set aside.
• In a large mixing bowl, combine cake mix, eggs, water, oil, sour cream, and vanilla extract. Beat at medium speed with an electric mixer for 2 minutes, scraping down sides of bowl as necessary.
• Pour into prepared pan, and level with a spatula. Tap pan on countertop to release air bubbles.
• Bake until golden brown around edges and a wooden pick inserted in center comes out clean, 11 to 12 minutes. Let cool completely in pan.
• Cover, and freeze until cake is firm enough to cut easily, approximately 1 hour.
• Meanwhile, in the workbowl of a food processor, process coconut, pulsing until finely minced. Set aside.
• Using a 2½-inch round cutter, cut 24 rounds from cake.
• Spread Dark Chocolate Filling on tops of 12 cake rounds. Top each with 4 almonds. Top each with another cake round. Spread Fluffy Vanilla Frosting on tops and sides of cakes. Lightly press minced coconut onto sides of cakes.
• Garnish with edible flowers, if desired.

For testing purposes, we used Duncan Hines White Cake mix.

†Refer to teatimemagazine.com/extras for more information.

Dark Chocolate Filling

Yield: ½ cup
Preparation: 5 minutes
Cook: 2 minutes
Refrigerate: 15 minutes or more

⅓ cup dark chocolate morsels
⅓ cup heavy whipping cream

• Place chocolate morsels in a small heatproof bowl. Set aside.
• In a small saucepan, scald cream, but do not boil. Pour over chocolate morsels, and let sit for 1 to 2 minutes to melt chocolate. Stir until smooth.
• Refrigerate, stirring every 15 minutes to check consistency. When filling thickens to desired consistency, spread on cakes.

Fluffy Vanilla Frosting

Yield: 3 cups
Preparation: 10 minutes

1 cup salted butter, softened
3 cups confectioners' sugar
1 teaspoon vanilla extract
2 tablespoons whole milk
1 cup marshmallow crème*

• In a large mixing bowl, combine butter, confectioners' sugar, vanilla extract, and milk. Beat at high speed with an electric mixer until mixture is light and fluffy, scraping down sides of bowl as necessary, approximately 2 minutes. Add marshmallow crème, beating just until incorporated.
• Use immediately.

For testing purposes, we used Marshmallow Fluff.

Sugared flowers dress up even the simplest of desserts. Many edible blossoms can be found in your own backyard, such as violas, pansies, and roses. When using flowers as a garnish, be sure to select those that are nonpoisonous and are pesticide and fertilizer free.

*"May this tea be steeped with love
For friendships sent down from above."*

—Sandy Lynam Clough

Mother's
DAY

MENU

Jasmine Rice Mini Muffins
Vanilla-Bean Fruit Salad
☕ *China Lin Yun Downy White Tea*

Sherried Crab Canapés
Italian Chicken & Pasta Salad
☕ *Kenya Organic Green Tea*

Earl Grey–Infused Chocolate Pots de Crème
Butter-Pecan Mini Sandwich Cookies
Apricot-Almond Tarts
☕ *Duke Cardiff Blend Black Tea*

Add egg mixture to flour mixture, stirring just until ingredients are combined.
• Fill wells of prepared pan three-fourths full.
• Bake until muffins are puffed and light brown, approximately 10 minutes.
• Remove muffins from pan. Serve immediately, or let cool and serve at room temperature.

*For testing purposes, we used Bob's Red Mill White Rice Flour.

†We used a Calphalon 24-well mini muffin pan. Wells have a 3-tablespoon capacity, which is a bit more than that of other brands. Using another brand may result in leftover batter.

Vanilla-Bean Fruit Salad
Yield: 8 servings
Preparation: 15 minutes
Cook: 5 minutes
Refrigerate: 4 hours

2 cups water
2 cups sugar
1 vanilla bean, split in half lengthwise, scraped, and seeds and pod reserved
2 cups honeydew melon balls
1 cup strawberry halves
1 cup fresh pineapple chunks
Garnish: toasted coconut

• In a small saucepan, combine water, sugar, and reserved vanilla bean seeds and pod. Cook over medium heat, whisking just until sugar dissolves. Remove from heat, and cool completely. Strain though cheesecloth, discarding solids. Set syrup aside.
• In a medium bowl, combine melon, strawberries, and pineapple.
• Pour syrup over fruit. Toss fruit to coat with syrup. Cover, and refrigerate until cold, approximately 4 hours.
• Garnish individual servings with toasted coconut, if desired.

The supreme vanilla flavor of this fruit salad comes from infusing the simple syrup with the split pod and scraped seeds of a vanilla bean. When purchasing vanilla beans, look for pods that are plump, slightly moist, and highly fragrant.

Jasmine Rice Mini Muffins
Yield: 24 muffins
Preparation: 15 minutes
Bake: 10 minutes

½ cup white rice flour*
1 teaspoon baking powder
1 teaspoon salt
1 tablespoon firmly packed brown sugar
3 large eggs
1 cup whole buttermilk
2 tablespoons salted butter, melted
1 cup cooked jasmine rice

• Preheat oven to 425°.
• Lightly coat a 24-well mini muffin pan† with nonstick cooking spray. Set aside.
• In a medium bowl, combine rice flour, baking powder, salt, and brown sugar, stirring to combine. Set aside.
• In another medium bowl, combine eggs, buttermilk, melted butter, and rice, stirring until combined.

Sherried Crab Canapés

Yield: 24 canapés
Preparation: 45 minutes
Bake: 7 minutes
Cook: 5 minutes
Broil: 2 to 3 minutes

6 tablespoons butter, melted and divided
24 slices white sandwich bread*
1 tablespoon all-purpose flour
½ cup whole milk
2 teaspoons sherry cooking wine

1 tablespoon finely diced pimiento
1 tablespoon chopped fresh chives
¼ teaspoon salt
⅛ teaspoon ground white pepper
½ cup fresh, pasteurized lump crabmeat
¼ cup panko bread crumbs
Garnish: hot paprika and diced pimiento

• Preheat oven to 350°.
• Using a pastry brush, coat wells of a 24-well mini muffin pan with 2 tablespoons melted butter. Set aside.
• Using a rolling pin, roll bread slices to a ⅛-inch thickness.

Using a 2¼-inch flower-shaped cutter, cut 24 flower shapes from bread. Discard crusts.

• Lightly press a bread flower into each prepared well of pan. Brush with 2 tablespoons melted butter.

• Bake until edges are golden brown, approximately 7 minutes. Remove bread cups to wire racks, and let cool completely. Store in an airtight container, and use the same day.

• Preheat broiler.

• In a small sauté pan, heat 1 tablespoon butter over medium-high heat. Add flour, whisking until smooth. Reduce heat to low, and cook mixture for 1 to 2 minutes but don't let brown. Add milk, whisking until smooth. Add sherry, pimiento, chives, salt, and white pepper, whisking to incorporate.

• Add crabmeat, stirring to combine. Cook over low heat until heated through.[†] Divide mixture among bread cups. Set aside.

• In a small bowl, combine bread crumbs and remaining 1 tablespoon melted butter. Sprinkle over crab mixture in bread cups. Place bread cups on a baking sheet.

• Broil just until bread crumbs are lightly browned.

• Garnish with paprika and pimiento, if desired.

• Serve immediately.

For testing purposes, we used Pepperidge Farm White Sandwich Bread.

†At this point crab mixture can be stored in the refrigerator. To reheat, place in a small nonstick pan, and add milk, 1 teaspoon at a time, if moisture is needed. Cook over low heat until warm and creamy.

NOTE: For freshness, crab should be cooked and consumed the day it is made. To prevent sogginess, tart shells should be filled just before broiling and serving.

Italian Chicken & Pasta Salad

Yield: 8 servings
Preparation: 25 minutes
Cook: 7 minutes

4 cups mini farfalle pasta*
¼ cup butter, melted
¼ cup fresh lemon juice
1 to 2 teaspoons Italian seasoning
2 cups chopped rotisserie chicken

½ cup chopped sun-dried tomatoes packed in oil, drained
½ cup loosely packed fresh shredded basil
½ cup crumbled goat cheese
Garnish: fresh basil leaves and lemon slices

• Cook pasta according to package directions, including the use of salt.[†] Cook to desired tenderness. Drain.

• In a large bowl, combine pasta with melted butter and lemon juice, tossing to coat pasta. Add 1 teaspoon Italian seasoning, tossing to evenly distribute seasoning. Taste, and add remaining 1 teaspoon Italian seasoning, if desired.

• Add chicken, sun-dried tomatoes, basil, and goat cheese, stirring and tossing lightly to incorporate.

• Garnish individual servings with basil leaves and lemon slices, if desired.

• Serve at room temperature.

For testing purposes, we used Barilla mini farfalle.

†Pasta may be cooked, rinsed in cold water, drained, cooled, covered, and refrigerated a day in advance. To reheat, add pasta to a large pot of boiling water. Turn off heat, and let sit for 1 minute. Drain, and continue with recipe, tossing with melted butter, lemon juice, and seasoning.

Earl Grey–Infused Chocolate Pots de Crème

Yield: 10 (2.75-ounce) servings
Preparation: 20 minutes
Cook: 2 to 3 minutes
Bake: 20 minutes
Refrigerate: 4 hours

4 ounces bittersweet chocolate, finely chopped*
1½ cups heavy whipping cream
4 bags Earl Grey tea
4 large egg yolks
¼ cup sugar
1½ teaspoons vanilla extract
1 recipe Orange-Scented Whipped Cream (recipe follows)

• Preheat oven to 300°.
• Place chocolate in a medium heatproof bowl. Set aside.
• In a small saucepan, scald cream, but do not let boil.
• Remove from heat, add tea bags, and steep for 15 minutes. Remove and discard tea bags.
• Heat infused cream just to a boil, and pour over chocolate. Let sit for 1 minute to melt chocolate. Stir until smooth and creamy. Set aside.
• In a small bowl, combine egg yolks, sugar, and vanilla extract, whisking until pale yellow, 2 to 3 minutes.
• Gradually add ¼ cup chocolate mixture to egg mixture to temper, whisking until combined. Add another ¼ cup chocolate mixture, whisking until combined. Add egg mixture to remaining chocolate mixture, whisking until combined.
• Divide mixture evenly among 10 (2.75-ounce) ramekins.†
• Place a clean, folded dish towel in the bottom of a baking dish or roasting pan large enough to hold ramekins. Place filled ramekins on top of dish towel. Carefully add water to baking dish so water level comes halfway up sides of ramekins.
• Bake until set, approximately 20 minutes. (Center may have a slight jiggle.)
• Carefully remove cups from water bath. Let cool completely, cover, and refrigerate until cold, at least 4 hours and up to 1 day.
• Transfer Orange-Scented Whipped Cream to a pastry bag fitted with a large open-star tip. Pipe cream onto cold pots de crème before serving.

For testing purposes, we used Ghirardelli 60% Cacao Bittersweet Chocolate.

†For easier pouring, transfer mixture to a large liquid-measuring cup, if desired.

Orange-Scented Whipped Cream

Yield: 2 cups
Preparation: 5 minutes

1 cup cold heavy whipping cream
3 tablespoons confectioners' sugar
1 teaspoon fresh orange zest
⅛ teaspoon orange extract

• In a medium bowl, beat cream at high speed with an electric mixer until beginning to thicken, 1 to 2 minutes. Add confectioners' sugar, orange zest, and orange extract, beating until incorporated and stiff peaks form.
• Use immediately, or cover and store in refrigerator until ready to use.

Butter-Pecan Mini Sandwich Cookies

Yield: 60 sandwich cookies
Preparation: 40 minutes
Freeze: 4 hours
Bake: 10 minutes per batch
Cool: 1 hour

½ cup salted butter, softened
¼ cup sugar
¼ cup firmly packed brown sugar
1 large egg
2 teaspoons vanilla, butter, and nut flavoring*
1¾ cup all-purpose flour
¼ teaspoon baking powder
½ teaspoon salt
⅓ cup finely chopped toasted pecans
1 recipe Toasted Pecan Buttercream (recipe follows)

• In a medium mixing bowl, combine butter, sugar, and brown sugar. Beat at high speed with an electric mixer until light and fluffy, 1 to 2 minutes. Add egg and flavoring, beating to combine. Set aside.
• In a small bowl, combine flour, baking powder, and salt, whisking well. Add to butter mixture, beating just until ingredients are well combined. Add pecans, stirring well.
• Divide dough into 2 portions. Roll each portion into a 1-inch diameter cylinder on plastic wrap. Wrap firmly, and secure to make airtight. Freeze for 4 hours or overnight.
• Preheat oven to 350°.

- Line 2 baking sheets with parchment paper. Set aside.
- Unwrap frozen cookie dough. Cut into ¼-inch slices. Place 1 inch apart on prepared baking sheets.
- Bake until cookies are firm and light golden brown around edges, approximately 10 minutes. Remove to wire racks, and let cool completely, approximately 1 hour.
- Transfer Toasted Pecan Buttercream to a pastry bag fitted with a small open-star tip. Pipe buttercream onto bottom of a cookie, then top with another cookie, placing flat bottoms together and pressing down lightly while twisting slightly to evenly distribute buttercream.
- Store cookies in an airtight container in the refrigerator for up to 3 days.

For testing purposes, we used McCormick Vanilla Butter & Nut Flavor.

Toasted Pecan Buttercream

Yield: ½ cup
Preparation: 5 minutes

¼ cup salted butter, softened
1 cup confectioners' sugar
¼ teaspoon vanilla extract
2 teaspoons whole milk
¼ cup finely chopped toasted pecans

- In a small bowl, combine butter, confectioners' sugar, vanilla extract, and milk. Beat at low speed with an electric mixer, gradually increasing speed to high, until light and fluffy. Add toasted pecans, stirring to combine.
- Use immediately, or cover and store in refrigerator. Let come to room temperature before using.

Guests will get the royal treatment when they have afternoon tea on Herend's Royal Garden *china custom designed for Prince William and his bride, Kate Middleton. Elegant brooches pinned to satin ribbon double as napkin rings and delightful party favors.*

Apricot-Almond Tarts

Yield: 8 (4-inch) tarts
Preparation: 30 minutes
Refrigerate: 30 minutes
Bake: 13 to 14 minutes
Cool: 1 hour

1 (14.1-ounce) package refrigerated pie dough
  (2 sheets)
⅔ cup plus ½ cup toasted slivered almonds, divided
⅓ cup sugar
1 tablespoon firmly packed light brown sugar
6 tablespoons salted butter
1 large egg
½ teaspoon vanilla extract
1½ tablespoons all-purpose flour
1 (30-ounce) can unpeeled apricot halves in heavy
  syrup, drained
½ cup apricot jam

• Preheat oven to 375°.
• Unroll pie dough on a lightly floured surface. Using a 4½-inch round cutter, cut 8 circles from pie dough. Press dough circles into 8 (4-inch) tart pans (1-inch deep) with removable bottoms. Refrigerate for 30 minutes.

• In the workbowl of a food processor, combine ⅔ cup toasted almonds and sugars. Process until almonds are ground and mixture resembles coarse sand. Add butter, egg, vanilla extract, and flour, and process until ingredients are incorporated and mixture is smooth.
• Divide almond mixture among prepared tart pans, spreading to smooth. Evenly top with remaining ½ cup toasted almonds.
• Bake tarts until mixture is set and slightly puffed, 13 to 14 minutes. Let cool completely on wire racks, approximately 1 hour. (Tarts will fall as they cool).
• Blot apricots dry on paper towels. Using a small, sharp knife, cut apricots vertically into ½-inch slices. Set aside.
• When tarts are completely cool, remove from pans. Arrange apricot slices decoratively in a swirled floral design on top of each tart.
• In a small saucepan, melt apricot jam over low heat, stirring until smooth. Using a pastry brush, coat apricots with jam. Serve immediately, or keep at room temperature until ready to serve.

NOTE: For best taste and texture, tarts should be made the same day they will be eaten. If they are refrigerated or made a day ahead, they will become gummy and soggy.

Birthday

MENU
Blueberry-Basil Scones
🍵 *Meyer Lemon Black Tea*

Creamy Tomato Soup
Orzo Salad Parmesan Baskets
Turkey & Ham Club Sandwiches
🍵 Spinach & Mushroom Phyllo Lasagna
Gyokuro Green Tea

Hazelnut French Macarons
Fruit-Topped Coconut Cream Tartlets
Lemon Mini Cupcakes
🍵 *Oriental Beauty Oolong Tea*

Blueberry-Basil Scones

Yield: 12 scones
Preparation: 20 minutes
Bake: 10 to 11 minutes

2 cups self-rising soft wheat flour*
2 tablespoons sugar
2½ teaspoons fresh lemon zest, divided
5 tablespoons cold salted butter
2 tablespoons minced fresh basil
¾ cup cold heavy whipping cream
½ cup fresh blueberries
½ cup plus 1 tablespoon confectioners' sugar
2 tablespoons fresh lemon juice
Garnish: fresh blueberries and fresh basil

• Preheat oven to 400°.
• Line a baking sheet with parchment paper. Set aside.
• In a medium bowl, combine flour, sugar, and 2 tea-spoons lemon zest, whisking until combined. Using a pastry blender, cut butter into flour mixture until mixture resembles coarse crumbs. Add basil, stirring to combine. Add cream, stirring until mixture forms a soft dough. (If mixture seems dry, add more cream, 1 tablespoon at a time, until a dough forms).
• On a lightly floured surface, knead dough lightly 3 times. Roll out to a ½-inch thickness.
• Scatter ¼ cup blueberries on half of dough. Fold other half of dough over blueberries to enclose them. Lightly roll out dough again to a ½-inch thickness. Repeat scattering, folding, and rolling process for remaining ¼ cup blueberries.

• Using a 2¼-inch round cutter, cut 12 scones from dough, rerolling scraps as little as possible. Place scones 2 inches apart on prepared baking sheets.
• Bake until edges are light golden brown, 10 to 11 minutes. Remove to a wire rack.
• In a small bowl, combine confectioners' sugar, lemon juice, and remaining ½ teaspoon lemon zest, whisking until smooth.
• Spoon glaze over scones, letting glaze drip down sides.
• Garnish with fresh blueberries and basil, if desired.

For testing purposes, we used White Lily Enriched Bleached Self-Rising Flour, available in grocery stores throughout the Southeastern United States and online at whitelily.com.

Creamy Tomato Soup

Yield: 1½ quarts
Preparation: 10 minutes
Cook: 20 minutes

1 tablespoon salted butter
2 tablespoons chopped shallot
2 (28-ounce) cans peeled tomatoes*
2 teaspoons smoked paprika
½ teaspoon salt
¼ teaspoon ground black pepper
½ cup heavy whipping cream
⅓ cup blue cheese crumbles
⅓ cup crumbled cooked bacon

• In a large saucepan, melt butter over medium-high heat. Add shallot, and reduce heat to low. Cook until soft, stirring occasionally, 2 to 3 minutes. Add tomatoes, paprika, salt, and pepper, and bring to a boil. Reduce heat, and simmer, covered, for 15 minutes.
• Remove from heat, and add cream.
• Using a hand-held immersion blender, blend to a very smooth consistency. Adjust seasoning by adding more salt and pepper, if desired.
• Divide blue cheese and bacon among individual servings.
• Serve warm.

For testing purposes, we used Cento San Marzano tomatoes, which are prized for their sweetness. A different type of tomato may be substituted.

Orzo Salad Parmesan Baskets

Yield: 8 servings
Preparation: 20 minutes
Cook: 5 to 7 minutes per batch

2 cups shredded Parmesan cheese
½ teaspoon olive oil
1 cup diced orange bell pepper
1 cup diced zucchini
¼ teaspoon garlic salt
1 cup cooked orzo pasta
⅓ cup canned garbanzo beans, drained
1 tablespoon chopped fresh chives
1 tablespoon chopped fresh parsley
⅓ cup toasted pine nuts
1 recipe Red-Wine-Honey Vinaigrette (recipe follows)
Garnish: fresh chives

• Preheat oven to 350°.
• Line several baking sheets with silicone baking mats or parchment paper.
• Sprinkle ¼ cup Parmesan cheese in a 4-inch circle on prepared baking sheets, no more than 3 per sheet.
• Bake until melted and golden brown around edges, 5 to 7 minutes per batch.
• Using a flat-edged utensil, quickly remove cheese circles from baking sheet, and drape each over the back of a well of a muffin pan. Let cool completely.
• In a medium nonstick sauté pan, heat olive oil over medium-high heat. Add bell pepper, zucchini, and garlic salt. Cook, stirring and tossing, until slightly charred and tender, approximately 5 minutes.
• In a medium bowl, combine zucchini mixture with orzo, garbanzo beans, chives, parsley, and pine nuts, stirring well. Set aside.
• Remove cheese baskets from muffin pan. Fill baskets with orzo salad, and drizzle with Red-Wine-Honey Vinaigrette.
• Garnish with fresh chives, if desired.
• Serve salad at room temperature.

Red-Wine-Honey Vinaigrette

Yield: ½ cup
Preparation: 10 minutes

¼ cup red-wine vinegar
3 tablespoons olive oil
¼ teaspoon salt
1 teaspoon honey
½ teaspoon minced shallot

• In a small bowl, combine red-wine vinegar, olive oil, salt, honey, and shallot, whisking well.

Turkey & Ham Club Sandwiches

Yield: 8 tea sandwiches
Preparation: 20 minutes

1 recipe Green Olive Aïoli (recipe follows)
6 slices toasted white sandwich bread*
16 spring mix lettuce leaves
8 very thin slices deli turkey
16 thin slices Campari tomatoes†
2 slices white American cheese
8 very thin slices deli ham
Garnish: pimiento-stuffed green olive quarters

• Spread Green Olive Aïoli on 1 side of each bread slice.
• On aïoli side of 1 bread slice, layer 4 lettuce leaves, 4 turkey slices arranged in a ruffled fashion, 4 tomato slices, and 1 cheese slice. Top with a bread slice, aïoli side down. Spread aïoli on upper side of bread. Top with 4 lettuce leaves, 4 ham slices arranged in a ruffled fashion, 4 tomato slices, and 1 bread slice, aïoli side down. Repeat with remaining ingredients.
• Using a sharp serrated or electric knife, cut crusts from all sides of sandwiches. Discard scraps. Cut each sandwich diagonally into quarters, creating 4 triangles.
• Garnish with an olive quarter, and secure with a frilled toothpick, if desired.

For testing purposes, we used Pepperidge Farm White Sandwich Bread.

†*If Campari tomatoes are not available, cherry tomatoes may be used instead.*

Green Olive Aïoli

Yield: ⅓ cup
Preparation: 10 minutes

⅓ cup mayonnaise
2 teaspoons fresh lemon juice
1 tablespoon finely minced green olives

• In a small bowl, combine mayonnaise, lemon juice, and olives, stirring well. Cover, and refrigerate until needed.

Spinach & Mushroom Phyllo Lasagna

Yield: 9 servings
Preparation: 1 hour
Cook: 20 minutes
Bake: 55 to 65 minutes

3 cups sliced white button mushrooms (¼-inch slices)
1 tablespoon olive oil
¼ teaspoon salt
⅛ teaspoon ground black pepper
¾ cup plus 2 tablespoons butter, divided
1 cup sliced leeks, white part only (¼-inch slices)
1 tablespoon water
2 (6-ounce) bags fresh baby spinach
¼ cup all-purpose flour
2¼ cups whole milk
½ teaspoon grated nutmeg
¼ teaspoon ground white pepper
1 (16-ounce) package frozen phyllo dough, thawed
1 cup grated Gruyère cheese
1 cup shredded sharp provolone cheese
1 cup grated Parmesan cheese
2 teaspoons fresh lemon zest
Garnish: roasted mushroom slices and fried spinach leaves*

• Preheat oven to 350°.
• Line a rimmed baking sheet with parchment paper. Set aside.
• In a medium bowl, toss mushrooms with olive oil. Spread mushrooms in a single layer on prepared baking sheet, and sprinkle with salt and pepper.
• Bake until mushrooms are tender and release juices, approximately 20 minutes.
• In a small sauté pan, melt 1 tablespoon butter over medium-high heat. Add leeks, and cook, stirring occasionally, until slightly charred, 2 to 3 minutes.

• Add water, cover pan, and reduce heat to low. Cook, stirring occasionally, until leeks are tender and translucent with light brown edges, approximately 8 minutes.
• Meanwhile, place spinach leaves in a colander, rinse with cold water, and shake dry.
• Heat a large nonstick sauté pan over high heat. Add spinach, and cook, stirring and tossing constantly, until spinach is wilted and tender, 1 to 2 minutes. Remove spinach to a bowl to cool. When cool enough to handle, squeeze excess liquid from spinach. Set spinach aside, and discard liquid.
• In a large sauté pan, melt ¼ cup butter over medium heat. Add flour, and cook, whisking constantly, for 1 to 2 minutes. (If flour begins to brown, reduce heat.) Add milk, whisking constantly until mixture thickens. Add nutmeg and white pepper, whisking to combine. Keep warm.
• Melt remaining ½ cup and 1 tablespoon butter. Brush a 9-inch square baking pan with 1 tablespoon melted butter. Set aside.
• Cut phyllo dough into 9-x-9-inch sheets. Layer 10 phyllo sheets in bottom of pan, brushing each layer lightly with melted butter. (Keep phyllo dough covered with a damp towel and plastic wrap as you work.)
• Spread one-third of mushrooms and one-third of spinach over phyllo layer in prepared pan. Add one-third of cheeses, then sprinkle with one-third of lemon zest. Spread one-third of warm white sauce over lemon layer. Layer 4 sheets phyllo over white sauce layer, brushing lightly with butter between each sheet. Repeat layers twice, ending with phyllo, and making sure to brush each phyllo sheet with butter. Brush last phyllo sheet with additional butter to prevent drying out.†
• Very lightly sprinkle phyllo with water. Using a sharp knife, score top layer of phyllo into 9 pieces.
• Bake uncovered until top is deep golden brown and cheese is bubbling, 35 to 45 minutes. Let cool for at least 15 minutes before cutting and serving.
• Garnish with roasted mushroom slices and fried spinach leaves, if desired.

*To fry spinach leaves, heat 1 inch vegetable oil in a small but deep saucepan until hot. Fry a few spinach leaves at a time until they become deep green and translucent. Drain on paper towels. (May be done early in the day and stored, lightly covered, at room temperature.)

†At this point, lasagna may be covered and refrigerated for up to 1 day until ready to bake.

Hazelnut French Macarons

Yield: 48 sandwich cookies
Preparation: 5 hours
Bake: 15 minutes per batch

3 egg whites
1 cup chopped hazelnuts with skins, toasted
2 cups confectioners' sugar*, divided
½ teaspoon vanilla extract
2 tablespoons sugar
1 recipe Dark Chocolate Ganache (recipe follows)

• Place egg whites in a medium mixing bowl, and let sit at room temperature, uncovered, for exactly 3 hours. (Aging the egg whites in this manner is essential to creating perfect macarons.)
• Line several baking sheets with parchment paper. Using a pencil, draw 1¼-inch circles 2 inches apart on parchment paper. Turn parchment paper over. Set aside.
• In the work bowl of a food processor, combine hazelnuts and 1 tablespoon confectioners' sugar, pulsing until very finely ground. (Don't overprocess or a nut butter will be created. The nut particles should stay separate and dry, not clump together.) Add remaining confectioners' sugar, and process just until combined. Set aside.
• Add vanilla extract to aged egg whites. Beat at medium-high speed with an electric mixer until frothy. Gradually add sugar, beating at high speed until stiff peaks form, 3 to 5 minutes. (Egg whites will be thick, creamy, and shiny.)
• Add hazelnut mixture to egg whites, folding gently until well combined. Let batter sit for 15 minutes.
• Transfer batter to a pastry bag fitted with a medium round tip. Pipe batter into drawn circles on prepared baking sheets.
• Slam pans vigorously on the counter 5 to 7 times to release air bubbles.
• Let sit at room temperature for 45 to 60 minutes before baking to help develop the macaron's signature crisp exterior when baked. (Macarons should feel dry to the touch and should not stick to finger.)
• Preheat oven to 275°.
• Bake until firm to the touch, approximately 15 minutes.
• Let cool completely on pans, and then remove to air-tight containers. Refrigerate until ready to fill and serve.
• Place Dark Chocolate Ganache in a pastry bag fitted with a small round tip. Pipe ganache onto flat side of macaron, and top with another macaron, flat sides together, pushing down lightly and twisting so filling will spread to edges.

*To measure confectioners' sugar accurately, spoon lightly into measuring cup, and level off with a straight edge. Do not pack or scoop sugar into cup as this will negatively affect final product.

NOTE: Dark Chocolate Ganache is the recommended filling, but other fillings, such as buttercream, lemon curd, or jam, may be substituted.

Dark Chocolate Ganache

Yield: ¾ cup
Preparation: 5 minutes
Cool: 30 minutes

½ cup heavy whipping cream
½ cup dark chocolate morsels*

• Place chocolate in a heatproof bowl. Set aside.
• In a small saucepan, scald cream, but do not boil. Pour over chocolate. Let sit for a few minutes to melt chocolate. Stir until smooth.
• Cool until slightly thick, approximately 30 minutes. (Refrigerate to speed up cooling process, if desired. Check every 10 minutes to make sure ganache is not solidifying.) Mixture is then ready to pipe onto macarons.

*For testing purposes, we used Ghirardelli 60% Cacao Bittersweet Chocolate Baking Chips.

"Come for tea . . . These words prompt lovely thoughts of time whiled away in the company of friends and family, tasty morsels to savor, and the bracing warmth of hot tea steeped to perfection and poured by a loving hand from a favorite pot into cups, porcelain thin."

—Barbara Cockerham

Fruit-Topped Coconut Cream Tartlets

Yield: 8 tartlets
Preparation: 30 minutes
Bake: 8 minutes
Refrigerate: 4 hours

½ cup sugar
½ cup water
1 recipe Coconut Cream (recipe follows)
1 recipe Graham-Cracker Tartlet Shells (recipe follows)
1 cup fresh raspberries
1 cup fresh blueberries
Garnish: fresh mint leaves

• In a small saucepan, combine sugar and water. Bring to a simmer to dissolve sugar, whisking occasionally. Let simple syrup cool completely.
• Divide Coconut Cream evenly among tartlet shells.
• Toss blueberries and raspberries in simple syrup. Arrange berries decoratively on top of Coconut Cream.
• Garnish each tartlet with mint, if desired.

Coconut Cream

Yield: 1½ cups
Preparation: 5 minutes
Cook: 3 to 4 minutes

⅓ cup sugar
2 tablespoons all-purpose flour
¼ teaspoon salt
1¼ cups canned coconut milk

• In a small saucepan, combine sugar, flour, salt, and coconut milk, whisking well. Bring just to a simmer over medium heat, whisking constantly. When mixture comes to a simmer and thickens, remove from heat.
• Transfer coconut cream to a heatproof bowl. Cover surface of coconut cream with plastic wrap to prevent a skin from forming.
• Refrigerate until cold, at least 4 hours and up to 1 day.

Graham-Cracker Tartlet Shells

Yield: 8 tartlet shells
Preparation: 15 minutes
Bake: 8 minutes
Cool: 1 hour
Freeze: 5 minutes

1 cup graham-cracker crumbs
2 tablespoons sugar
¼ cup butter, melted
1 egg white, lightly beaten

• Preheat oven to 350°.
• In a medium bowl, combine graham-cracker crumbs, sugar, and butter, stirring to combine. Add egg white, stirring until mixture is uniformly moist.
• Divide crumb mixture evenly among 8 (2½-inch) tartlet pans, pressing crumbs into bottom and up sides of each pan.
• Bake until firm and light brown, approximately 8 minutes. Let cool completely in pans. Freeze for 5 minutes before attempting to remove tartlet shells from pans. For best taste and texture, use within 24 hours.

Lemon Mini Cupcakes

Yield: 24 mini cupcakes
Preparation: 20 minutes
Bake: 12 minutes

1¼ cups all-purpose flour
1¼ teaspoons baking powder
¼ teaspoon baking soda
¼ teaspoon salt
½ cup salted butter, softened
1 cup sugar
2 teaspoons fresh lemon zest
2 large eggs
½ cup whole buttermilk
2 tablespoons fresh lemon juice
1 recipe Lemon Buttercream (recipe follows)
1 recipe Springerle Fondant Cupcake Toppers
   (recipe follows)

"What better way to suggest friendliness—and to create it—than with a cup of tea?"

—J. Grayson Luttrell

• Preheat oven to 350°.
• Lightly coat a 24-well mini muffin pan* with nonstick cooking spray with flour. Set aside.
• In a small bowl, combine flour, baking powder, baking soda, and salt, whisking well. Set aside.
• In a large mixing bowl, combine butter, sugar, and lemon zest. Beat at high speed with an electric mixer for 5 minutes. Add eggs, beating to combine. Add flour mixture alternately with buttermilk and lemon juice, beginning and ending with flour mixture and scraping down sides of bowl occasionally. Fill wells of prepared muffin pan three-fourths full.
• Bake until wooden pick inserted in centers comes out clean, 12 to 13 minutes. Remove immediately to a wire rack. Let cool completely.
• Place Lemon Buttercream in a piping bag fitted with a large (Wilton #1M) open-star tip. Pipe buttercream onto each cupcake in decorative swirls.
• Top each cupcake with a fondant Springerle Cupcake Topper.

We used a Calphalon 24-well mini muffin pan. Wells have a 3-tablespoon capacity, which is a bit more than that of other brands. Using another brand may result in leftover batter.

Lemon Buttercream
Yield: 2¼ cups
Preparation: 10 minutes

3½ cups confectioners' sugar
1 cup salted butter, softened
1 teaspoon fresh lemon zest
2 tablespoons fresh lemon juice
1 teaspoon lemon extract
½ teaspoon salt
Yellow food coloring*

• In a medium mixing bowl, combine confectioners' sugar, butter, lemon zest, lemon juice, lemon extract, and salt. Beat at low speed with an electric mixer until ingredients are incorporated. Increase speed to high, beating until mixture is fluffy. Tint to desired color with food coloring.
• Use immediately, or store, covered, in the refrigerator.

Before using, bring to room temperature, and beat at high speed with an electric mixer for 1 minute.

For testing purposes, we used LorAnn "Egg" Yellow Liquid Food Color from Springerle Joy, springerlejoy.com or 412-616-9066.

Springerle Fondant Cupcake Toppers
Yield: 24 toppers
Preparation 30 minutes

White fondant
Yellow food coloring*
Luster dust‡

• Tint fondant to desired color with a few drops of food coloring, kneading until color is uniform. (To prevent hands from becoming stained, wear latex gloves.)
• Using a rolling pin and thickness guides, roll fondant to a 3-millimeter thickness.
• Line a tray or baking sheet with waxed paper. Set aside.
• Press assorted 2-inch flower Springerle molds† firmly and evenly into fondant to create design. Using a 1½-inch round cutter, cut out central designs. Carefully lift away excess fondant. (Fondant may be reused but must be placed in plastic wrap and sealed in a ziplock bag to prevent drying out.)
• Using a thin-bladed lifter, lift fondant circles onto prepared tray.
• Using a small paintbrush dipped in water, brush luster dust over designs on fondant circles. Let dry, then store toppers at room temperature in an airtight container. Use within 24 hours.

For testing purposes, we used LorAnn "Egg" Yellow Liquid Food Color from Springerle Joy, springerlejoy.com or 412-616-9066.

†*For testing purposes, we used Springerle Joy Lilies of the Valley (2201), Corn Flower (2204), and Carnation (2375) Springerle molds, springerlejoy.com or 412-616-9066.*

‡*For testing purposes, we used Wilton White Pearl Dust, wilton.com.*

Ordinary cupcakes become dazzling desserts with the addition of fondant cupcake toppers pressed in floral Springerle molds and brushed with a hint of pearl luster dust.

TEA CELEBRATIONS

Thanksgiving

MENU

Dilled Cheese Muffins
☕ *Organic Pai Mu Tan White Tea*

Creamy Sweet Potato Soup
Ham & Chutney Tea Sandwiches
Bacon, Leek & Swiss Quiche
☕ *Nepal Ilam Black Tea*

Chess Tartlets
Chocolate Mincemeat Cookies
Carrot-Pineapple Cakes
☕ *Tie Kuan Yin Oolong Tea*

Dilled Cheese Muffins

Yield: 12 muffins
Preparation: 10 minutes
Bake: 18 to 20 minutes

2 cups all-purpose flour
1 tablespoon sugar
1 tablespoon baking powder
1½ teaspoons dried dill
1 teaspoon dried minced onion
½ teaspoon salt
1 cup whole milk
¾ cup small curd cottage cheese
¼ cup butter, melted
1 large egg, lightly beaten

• Preheat oven to 350°.
• Spray a 12-well mini cheesecake pan* with nonstick cooking spray with flour.
• In a medium bowl, combine flour, sugar, baking powder, dill, onion, and salt, whisking well. Set aside.
• In another medium bowl, combine milk, cottage cheese, melted butter, and egg, stirring until incorporated. Add egg mixture to flour mixture, stirring just until a dough forms. (Overmixing will cause muffins to be tough.)
• Fill wells of prepared pan three-fourths full.
• Bake until lightly browned and a toothpick inserted into centers comes out clean, 18 to 20 minutes.

We used Chicago Metallic 12-well Mini Cheesecake Pans. Wells are 2 inches in diameter and 1½ inches deep and have removable bottoms.

For a decorative touch, wrap each Dilled Cheese Muffin with strips of parchment paper, and tie with thin orange ribbon. When served on a white dessert stand, these dainty, flavorful muffins add style to the Thanksgiving tea table.

Creamy Sweet Potato Soup

Yield: 1 quart
Preparation: 15 minutes
Bake: 60 to 90 minutes
Cook: 20 minutes

3 medium sweet potatoes
1 tablespoon olive oil
1 quart water
4 teaspoons vegetable base*
2 teaspoons fresh thyme leaves
½ cup heavy whipping cream
Garnish: crumbled blue cheese

• Preheat oven to 375°.
• Line a baking sheet with foil. Set aside.
• Pierce sweet potatoes with a knife, rub with olive oil, and place on prepared baking sheet.
• Bake until potatoes are very soft when squeezed, 60 to 90 minutes.
• Let cool slightly. Remove pulp, and discard skins.
• In a medium stockpot, bring water and vegetable base to a boil, whisking until base dissolves. Add sweet potato pulp and thyme.
• Cook over low heat for 15 minutes to develop flavor.
• Remove from heat, and add cream.
• Using an immersion blender, blend until very smooth. (Add more cream or vegetable broth, if necessary, to achieve desired consistency.)
• Garnish with crumbled blue cheese, if desired.

For testing purposes, we used Better Than Bouillon Vegetable Base.

While made from only a few ingredients, this simple tea sandwich (left) is packed with complex seasonal flavors. It is wise to incorporate into a tea menu at least one easy yet delicious recipe that can be assembled quickly if other dishes require a bit more preparation time.

Bacon, Leek & Swiss Quiche

Yield: 6 (4½-inch) quiches
Preparation: 20 minutes
Cook: 15 to 20 minutes
Bake: 20 to 22 minutes

1 tablespoon butter
1 tablespoon olive oil
2 cups sliced leeks (¼-inch slices)
1 (14.1-ounce) package refrigerated pie dough
   (2 sheets)
3 large eggs
1¼ cups heavy whipping cream
½ teaspoon salt
⅛ teaspoon ground black pepper
1½ cups coarsely shredded Swiss cheese
6 slices bacon, cooked and finely crumbled, divided

• Preheat oven to 350°.
• In a medium nonstick skillet, heat butter and olive oil over medium-high heat. Add leeks, and reduce heat to low, stirring occasionally. Cook until tender and caramelized, 15 to 20 minutes. Set aside.
• Unroll pie dough on a lightly floured surface. Using a 5-inch cutter, cut 6 circles from dough. Press circles lightly into bottoms and up sides of 6 (4½-inch) tart pans, trimming to fit, if necessary. Set aside.
• In a medium bowl, combine eggs, cream, salt, and pepper, whisking well. Set aside.
• Divide cheese, leeks, and bacon evenly among prepared tart pans. Divide egg mixture among tart pans. Place tart pans on a rimmed baking sheet.
• Bake until filling is set and slightly puffed, 20 to 22 minutes. Let quiches cool slightly. (Filling will fall as it cools). Carefully remove from pans.
• Serve warm or at room temperature.

Ham & Chutney Tea Sandwiches

Yield: 16 sandwiches
Preparation: 15 minutes

1 (8-ounce) package cream cheese, softened
¼ cup chutney*
1 tablespoon spicy mustard
8 very thin slices deli ham
8 slices honey wheat bread†

• In a small bowl, combine cream cheese, chutney, and mustard, stirring until smooth and blended. Spread 1 tablespoon cream-cheese mixture onto each bread slice. Top each of 4 bread slices (cream-cheese side up) with 2 ham slices, arranging ham in a ruffled pattern. Top each with another bread slice (cream-cheese side down).
• Using a sharp, serrated bread knife, trim crusts from sandwiches. Discard crusts. Cut each sandwich diagonally into quarters, forming 4 triangles. (Wipe knife as necessary to create a clean cut.)
• Cover with a slightly damp paper towel, and keep in an airtight container in the refrigerator until ready to serve.

*For testing purposes, we used Crosse & Blackwell Genuine Major Grey's Chutney.

†For testing purposes, we used Sara Lee Honey Wheat Bread.

NOTE: Sandwiches can be made early in the day.

Chess Tartlets

Yield: 12 tartlets
Preparation: 15 minutes
Bake: 13 to 15 minutes

1 (14.1-ounce) package refrigerated pie dough
   (2 sheets)
2 large eggs
½ cup sugar
¼ cup butter, melted
2 teaspoons cornmeal
1 tablespoon fresh lemon juice
⅛ teaspoon salt
Garnish: lemon zest curls

• Preheat oven to 325°.
• Unroll pie dough on a lightly floured surface. Using a 2½-inch square cutter, cut 12 squares from dough. Press a dough square lightly into each well of a 12-well square tartlet pan with removable bottoms*. Set aside.
• In a medium bowl, combine eggs, sugar, melted butter, cornmeal, lemon juice, and salt, whisking until incorporated. Divide batter evenly among tartlet shells.
• Bake until set, 13 to 15 minutes. Let cool completely on wire racks. Carefully remove tartlets from pan.
• Garnish tartlets with lemon zest curls, if desired.

For testing purposes, we used Chicago Metallic Lift & Serve Single Squares Pan.

Chocolate Mincemeat Cookies

Yield: 54 cookies
Preparation: 5 minutes
Refrigerate: 1 hour
Bake: 9 minutes per batch

½ cup plus 2 tablespoons all-purpose flour
½ teaspoon baking powder
¼ teaspoon salt
¼ teaspoon ground allspice
⅛ teaspoon baking soda
⅛ teaspoon ground cloves
⅛ teaspoon ground nutmeg
5 tablespoons salted butter, melted
2 ounces semisweet chocolate, melted
1 large egg
1 large egg yolk
½ cup firmly packed light brown sugar

1 teaspoon vanilla extract
1 cup bittersweet chocolate morsels*
¼ cup chopped dried cherries
2 tablespoons chopped dried figs
2 tablespoons chopped golden raisins

• Preheat oven to 350°.
• Line several baking sheets with parchment paper. Set aside.
• In a medium bowl, combine flour, baking powder, salt, allspice, baking soda, cloves, and nutmeg, whisking to combine. Set aside.
• In a small bowl, combine melted butter and melted chocolate, stirring well. Set aside to cool slightly.
• In a large bowl, combine egg and egg yolk, brown sugar, and vanilla extract, whisking well. Add cooled chocolate mixture, stirring well. Gradually add flour mixture, stirring until combined. Add chocolate morsels and dried fruit, stirring until incorporated.
• Cover and refrigerate dough until cold, approximately 1 hour.
• Using a levered 1-teaspoon scoop, drop dough 2 inches apart onto prepared baking sheets.
• Bake until cookies are set and light golden brown around edges, approximately 9 minutes per batch.
• Let cool for 1 minute on baking sheets, and then remove to wire racks to cool completely. Store in airtight containers.

• In a medium bowl, combine flour, cinnamon, baking soda, baking powder, and salt, whisking until blended. Set aside.
• In a large mixing bowl, combine eggs, oil, sugar, and flavoring. Beat at medium speed with an electric mixer until combined.
• Add flour mixture, beating at low speed until mixture is smooth. Add carrot and pineapple, stirring well. Pour batter into prepared baking pan, and level with a spatula.
• Bake until a toothpick inserted into center comes out clean, 15 to 16 minutes. Let cool completely in pan.
• Using a 2¾-inch round cutter, cut 20 circles from cake.
• Spread half of Mascarpone Frosting on 10 cake circles. Top each with a remaining cake circle. Spread remaining frosting on each.
• Garnish with chopped pistachios, if desired.
• Cover and refrigerate for up to a day until ready to serve.

*Vietnamese or Saigon cinnamon is a sweet-hot cinnamon. Regular cinnamon can be substituted, but the flavor will not be as pronounced. Vietnamese cinnamon is available from Penzeys Spices (penzeys.com). Look for Saigon cinnamon among McCormick's Spices or Spice Islands products on the grocery store's spice aisle.

†For testing purposes, we used McCormick's Imitation Vanilla Butter & Nut Flavor.

Carrot-Pineapple Cakes

Yield: 10 cakes
Preparation: 30 minutes
Bake: 15 to 16 minutes

2 cups all-purpose flour
2 teaspoons Vietnamese cinnamon*
2 teaspoons baking soda
2 teaspoons baking powder
½ teaspoon salt
3 large eggs
1 cup canola oil
1 cup sugar
1 teaspoon vanilla, butter, and nut flavoring†
3 cups very finely grated carrot
½ cup finely chopped dried pineapple
1 recipe Mascarpone Frosting (recipe follows)
Garnish: chopped salted, roasted pistachios

• Preheat oven to 350°.
• Spray a 17-x-12-inch baking pan with nonstick baking spray with flour. Line with parchment paper, and spray again. Set aside.

Mascarpone Frosting

Yield: 2¾ cups
Preparation: 10 minutes

4 cups confectioners' sugar
½ cup salted butter, softened
8 ounces mascarpone cheese
1 teaspoon vanilla extract
¼ cup heavy whipping cream
¼ teaspoon salt

• In a medium bowl, combine confectioners' sugar, butter, mascarpone cheese, vanilla extract, cream, and salt. Beat at medium speed with an electric mixer until mixture is smooth and creamy.
• Use immediately.

"The joy of a cultivated tea palate is the ability to savor a beverage we too often take for granted."

—Michael Harney

Christmas

MENU

Pepper-Asiago Scones
Crab Bisque
☕ *Dragonwell Green Tea*

Smoked Salmon Tea Sandwiches with Dill-Caper Butter
Turkey-Cranberry Crostini
Roast Pork Tenderloin Stack
☕ *Mrs. Grey's Blend Black Tea*

Eggnog Cheesecakes
Lemon Linzer Cookies
Chocolate-Toffee Layer Cakes
☕ *Almond Sugar Cookie Black Tea*

Pepper-Asiago Scones

Yield: 24 scones
Preparation: 20 minutes
Bake: 10 minutes

2¾ cups all-purpose flour
1 tablespoon sugar
3½ teaspoons baking powder
2 teaspoons freshly ground black pepper*, divided
½ teaspoon salt
¼ cup cold salted butter
1¼ cups freshly finely grated asiago cheese
1½ cups plus 2 tablespoons cold heavy whipping
   cream, divided

• Preheat oven to 425°.
• Line 2 baking sheets with parchment paper. Set aside.
• In a medium bowl, combine flour, sugar, baking powder, 1¾ teaspoons pepper, and salt, stirring well. Using a pastry blender, cut butter into flour mixture until mixture resembles coarse crumbs. Add cheese, stirring to combine. Add 1½ cups cream, and stir until a soft dough forms. Work dough with hands to bring together in bowl. (If mixture seems dry, add cream, 1 tablespoon at a time, until a dough forms.)
• Turn dough out onto a floured surface, and knead 3 to 4 times. Roll out to a ½-inch thickness.
• Using a 2-inch round cutter, cut 24 scones from dough, rerolling scraps as necessary. Place scones 2 inches apart on prepared baking sheets.
• Brush tops of scones with remaining 2 tablespoons cream, and sprinkle with remaining ¼ teaspoon pepper.
• Bake until edges are golden brown and a wooden pick inserted into centers comes out clean, approximately 10 minutes.

For testing purposes, we used freshly ground black pepper. Regular black pepper can be used, but the flavor will be more pronounced.

Crab Bisque

Yield: 1 quart
Preparation: 15 minutes
Cook: 35 to 40 minutes

¼ cup salted butter
½ cup minced celery

¼ cup minced shallots
¼ cup all-purpose flour
2 cups chicken broth
2 (8-ounce) bottles clam juice
1 small bay leaf
¼ teaspoon ground white pepper
¼ teaspoon ground nutmeg
¼ cup heavy whipping cream
1 cup fresh, pasteurized jumbo lump crabmeat, divided
Garnish: ground hot paprika

• In a medium saucepan, melt butter over medium-high heat. Add celery and shallots, and cook until tender, 2 to 3 minutes, reducing heat if browning occurs. Add flour, whisking to incorporate. Cook mixture for 2 to 3 minutes, but don't let brown. Add chicken broth and clam juice, stirring constantly, and bring to a boil. Reduce heat to low. Add bay leaf, white pepper, and nutmeg, stirring to incorporate.
• Cover saucepan, and cook for 30 minutes to develop flavor, stirring occasionally. Remove and discard bay leaf.
• Let cool until safe enough to place in the container of a blender. Add cream. Process on high speed until smooth and creamy.
• Return soup to saucepan. Add ¾ cup cup crabmeat, stirring to incorporate. Heat soup over low heat just until it comes to a simmer. Serve warm.
• Divide remaining ¼ cup crabmeat among individual servings.
• Garnish with hot paprika, if desired.

NOTE: Soup may be made one day in advance and gently reheated before serving.

• When ready to serve, using a sharp serrated knife, trim sandwiches to 4-x-3-inch rectangles. Cut each sandwich in half, then each half into 4 (2-x-¾-inch) slices, yielding 8 tea sandwiches. For best flavor, serve at slightly less than room temperature.

For testing purposes, we used Echo Falls Scottish Smoked Salmon.

Turkey-Cranberry Crostini

Yield: 16 crostini
Preparation: 30 minutes
Refrigerate: 4 hours

2 cups fresh cranberries
¼ cup sugar
2 tablespoons firmly packed brown sugar
½ teaspoon fresh orange zest
2 tablespoons fresh orange juice
1 tablespoon fresh lime juice
½ teaspoon fresh lime zest
2 tablespoons minced celery
2 tablespoons finely chopped toasted pecans
1 (8-ounce) package cream cheese, softened
16 French bread crostini
16 leaves spring mix lettuce
16 slices deli roast turkey

• In a small saucepan, combine cranberries, sugar, brown sugar, orange zest, orange juice, lime juice, and lime zest, stirring well. Bring to a boil over medium-high heat, stirring occasionally. Reduce heat to a simmer, and cook until mixture is thick, 3 to 5 minutes. Let cool to room temperature.
• Add celery and pecans, stirring to combine. Cover, and refrigerate until well chilled, at least 4 hours and up to 1 day.
• Place cream cheese in a piping bag fitted with a medium open-star tip. Pipe cream cheese onto each crostini, covering top surface. Place a lettuce leaf on top of cream-cheese layer of each crostini. Set aside.
• Firmly roll each turkey slice into a long cylinder. Using a sharp knife, cut 3 (¼-inch) slices from each cylinder, discarding scraps.
• Lay 3 slices on each crostini in a shingled fashion. Spoon or pipe ¼ teaspoon cranberry mixture between each turkey slice.
• Serve immediately.

Smoked Salmon Tea Sandwiches with Dill-Caper Butter

Yield: 16 sandwiches
Preparation: 20 minutes
Refrigerate: 2 hours

½ cup salted butter, softened
2 tablespoons chopped fresh dill
1 tablespoon chopped capers
6 slices pumpernickel bread, divided
1 (4-ounce) package thinly sliced smoked salmon*, divided

• In a small bowl, combine butter, dill, and capers, stirring well.
• Spread butter mixture on top sides of 2 bread slices. Top with half of smoked salmon.
• Spread butter mixture on both sides of 2 bread slices. Place a slice on top of each smoked-salmon layer. Top with remaining smoked salmon.
• Spread butter mixture on the top sides of remaining 2 bread slices. Place each, butter side down, atop smoked salmon.
• Cover sandwiches with slightly damp paper towels. For ease of cutting, place in a covered container, and refrigerate for 2 hours.

Roast Pork Tenderloin Stack

Yield: 8 servings
Preparation: 15 minutes
Bake: 20 minutes
Cook: 4 minutes per batch

1 (18.4-ounce) package pork tenderloins
   (2 tenderloins)
2 tablespoons olive oil
½ teaspoon garlic salt
¼ teaspoon ground black pepper
¼ teaspoon hot paprika
1 recipe Spicy Apricot Sauce (recipe follows)
1 recipe Polenta Cakes (recipe follows)
1 recipe Brussels Sprouts Slaw (recipe follows)

• Preheat oven to 350°.
• Line a baking pan with heavy-duty foil. Set aside.
• Trim silver skin from pork tenderloins, if necessary. Rub all over with olive oil. Sprinkle evenly with garlic salt, pepper, and paprika. Rub spices into meat. Place pork on prepared baking pan.
• Bake for 20 minutes. (Pork will be rare.)
• Carefully fold foil to encase pork and keep it moist. Cool until safe enough to handle.*
• Cut pork into ¼-inch slices. Coat with pork juices from pan.
• Heat a large nonstick sauté pan over medium-high heat. Cook pork for approximately 2 minutes per side to finish cooking and to caramelize exterior. (Meat should be medium brown on the outside but still tender and juicy.)
• Spoon Spicy Apricot Sauce onto centers of individual plates. Top each with a warm Polenta Cake. Arrange 3 pork slices on top of each Polenta Cake. Drizzle or brush pork with Spicy Apricot Sauce.
• Top each with Brussels Sprouts Slaw. Serve immediately.

Pork can be refrigerated at this point for up to 1 day.

Spicy Apricot Sauce

Yield: 2 cups
Preparation: 5 minutes
Cook: 5 minutes

2 (9.5-ounce) jars apricot jam*
¼ cup fresh lemon juice
¼ teaspoon red pepper flakes
¼ teaspoon ground black pepper
½ teaspoon salt

• In a small sauté pan, combine jam, lemon juice, red pepper flakes, black pepper, and salt, whisking well.
• Cook over low heat for 5 minutes to develop flavor. Serve warm.

For testing purposes, we used Dickinson's Purely Fruit Apricot Jam.

Polenta Cakes

Yield: 8 servings
Preparation: 15 minutes
Cook: 30 minutes

1 quart water
1 teaspoon salt
1½ cups coarse-grind polenta*
1 tablespoon fresh thyme leaves
2 tablespoons butter
2 tablespoons heavy whipping cream
½ teaspoon olive oil

• Butter a 13-x-9½-inch shallow rimmed pan. Set aside.
• In a deep medium saucepan, heat water and salt to boiling. Gradually add polenta and thyme, stirring constantly with a long-handled spoon. Reduce heat to low, and cook polenta for 15 to 20 minutes, stirring occasionally. Mixture will be very thick. Add more water, a few tablespoons at a time, if polenta becomes too firm.
• Remove from heat. Add butter and cream, stirring until ingredients are incorporated.

- Pour into prepared pan, and let sit until firm and cool enough to handle.[†]
- Using a 2¾-inch round cutter, cut 8 rounds from polenta cake.
- Heat olive oil in a large nonstick sauté pan over medium-high heat. Sear polenta cakes on each side until exterior is firm and crispy, approximately 3 minutes per side. Keep warm on a baking sheet in a low-temperature oven.

For testing purposes, we used Bob's Red Mill Corn Grits Also Known As Polenta.

[†]*At this point, polenta may be covered and refrigerated 1 day in advance. Let come to room temperature before pan searing.*

Brussels Sprouts Slaw
Yield: 2 cups
Preparation: 25 minutes
Cook: 1 minute
Refrigerate: 4 hours

1½ quarts water
2 cups fresh whole Brussels sprouts
¼ cup sherry vinegar
¼ cup olive oil
2 teaspoons sugar
1 teaspoon minced shallot
¼ teaspoon salt
¼ teaspoon ground black pepper
⅓ cup chopped red bell pepper slices

- In a medium saucepan, bring water to a boil over high heat. Add Brussels sprouts to boiling water, and cook for 1 minute.
- Immediately remove from boiling water, and place in an ice bath to stop cooking process. Drain well and cool.
- Slice Brussels sprouts in half vertically, then slice each half lengthwise into ⅛-inch slices. Set aside.
- In a small bowl, combine vinegar, olive oil, sugar, shallot, salt, and pepper, whisking well.
- In a medium nonreactive bowl, combine Brussels sprouts, bell pepper, and vinaigrette, stirring and tossing to coat.
- Cover, and refrigerate until cold, approximately 4 hours.
- Drain before serving.

Eggnog Cheesecakes
Yield: 12 cheesecakes
Preparation: 30 minutes
Bake: 17 to 18 minutes
Refrigerate: 4 hours

¾ cup gingersnap crumbs
¼ cup plus 2 teaspoons sugar, divided
2 tablespoons butter, melted
1 (8-ounce) package cream cheese, softened
1 large egg
3 teaspoons all-purpose flour
¼ cup eggnog
¼ teaspoon ground cinnamon
¼ teaspoon ground nutmeg
1 recipe Vanilla Whipped Cream (recipe on page 88)
Garnish: additional ground nutmeg

- Preheat oven to 350°.
- In a small bowl, combine gingersnap crumbs, 2 teaspoons sugar, and melted butter, stirring well. Divide evenly among wells of a 12-well mini cheesecake pan*.
- Bake until golden brown, 6 to 8 minutes. Remove to a wire rack, and let cool completely.
- In a medium bowl, beat cream cheese at high speed with an electric mixer until creamy and smooth. Add remaining ¼ cup sugar, egg, flour, eggnog, cinnamon, and nutmeg, beating just until incorporated. Divide mixture evenly among wells of prepared pan.
- Bake until cheesecakes are set and slightly puffed, 11 to 12 minutes.
- Let cool completely on a wire rack. Cover, and refrigerate for 4 hours or overnight.
- When ready to serve, remove cheesecakes from pans.
- Place Vanilla Whipped Cream in a piping bag fitted with a large open-star tip. Pipe whipped cream onto cheesecakes in a decorative swirl.
- Garnish with nutmeg, if desired.

We used Chicago Metallic 12-well Mini Cheesecake Pans. Wells are 2 inches in diameter and 1½ inches deep and have removable bottoms.

HELPFUL *Hint*

Add color and sparkle to your tea tray or dessert stand with sugared fruits and herbs. Here, we misted fresh cranberries and a sprig of rosemary with cooking spray and sprinkled them with superfine sugar.

Vanilla Whipped Cream

Yield: 3 cups
Preparation: 5 minutes

1½ cups cold heavy whipping cream
½ teaspoon vanilla extract
¼ cup confectioners' sugar

• In a small bowl, combine cream, vanilla extract, and confectioners' sugar. Beat at high speed with an electric mixer until thickened.
• Refrigerate in a covered container for up to 3 days.

Lemon Linzer Cookies

Yield: 24 sandwich cookies
Preparation: 1 hour
Refrigerate: 1 hour
Bake: 8 minutes per batch

½ cup salted butter, softened
⅓ cup sugar
½ teaspoon vanilla extract
1 large egg yolk
1 teaspoon heavy whipping cream
1½ cups all-purpose flour
¼ teaspoon salt
½ cup lemon curd*
Garnish: confectioners' sugar

• Preheat oven to 350°.
• Line 2 baking sheets with parchment paper. Set aside.
• In a medium mixing bowl, combine butter and sugar. Beat at high speed with an electric mixer until light and fluffy, 2 to 3 minutes. Add vanilla extract, egg yolk, and cream, beating until incorporated.
• In a small bowl, combine flour and salt. Add to butter mixture, beating just until incorporated.
• While dough is still in mixing bowl, bring dough together with hands. Turn dough out onto plastic wrap, and shape into a flat disk. Wrap tightly in plastic wrap, and refrigerate until dough is firm, approximately 1 hour.
• On a lightly floured surface, roll dough out to a ¼-inch thickness. Using a 1½-inch round cutter, cut 48 cookies from dough. Using a small diamond-shaped linzer cutter, cut a pattern into half of cookies, discarding diamond centers.
• Place cookies on prepared baking sheets.
• Bake until light golden brown, approximately 8 minutes. Remove to wire racks, and let cool completely.
• Spread a small amount of lemon curd on bottom of whole cookies. Top each with a cutout cookie.
• Store in an airtight container in the refrigerator until ready to use.
• Garnish with a dusting of confectioners' sugar, if desired.

*For testing purposes, we used Dickinson's Lemon Curd.

Chocolate-Toffee Layer Cakes

Yield: 16 cakes
Preparation: 1 hour
Refrigerate: 1 hour
Bake: 15 minutes
Freeze: 1 to 2 hours

1½ cups water
3 bags Earl Grey tea
10 tablespoons salted butter, softened
1¾ cups sugar
1½ teaspoons vanilla extract
2 large eggs
⅓ cup natural unsweetened cocoa powder*
2½ cups cake flour
1¼ teaspoons baking soda
½ teaspoon salt
½ cup dark chocolate morsels†
½ cup heavy whipping cream
1 recipe Chocolate Buttercream (recipe follows)
¼ cup toffee bits‡
Garnish: fresh raspberries and sugared thyme**

(Continued on page 90)

- Preheat oven to 350°.
- Line a 17-x-12-inch rimmed baking pan with parchment paper, and spray with nonstick cooking spray. Set aside.
- In a small saucepan, bring water to a boil. Remove from heat, and add tea bags. Cover, and steep for 5 minutes. Remove and discard tea bags. Let tea cool to room temperature.
- Refrigerate tea until cold, approximately 1 hour.
- In a large bowl, combine butter and sugar. Beat at high speed with an electric mixer until light and fluffy, 3 to 4 minutes. Add vanilla extract and eggs, beating until incorporated. Set aside.
- In a medium bowl, combine cocoa powder, flour, baking soda, and salt, whisking well. Add flour mixture to butter mixture alternately with cold tea, beginning and ending with flour mixture.
- Spread batter into prepared pan, smoothing into an even layer. Tap pan vigorously several times on countertop to remove air bubbles from batter.
- Bake until a wooden pick inserted in the center comes out clean, approximately 15 minutes.
- Remove pan to a wire rack, and let cool completely.
- Cover pan, and place in freezer until cake feels firm to the touch, 1 to 2 hours.
- Using a 2½-inch square cutter, cut 24 squares from cake. Cut each square in half horizontally, creating 2 layers. Set aside.
- Place chocolate morsels in a small heatproof bowl. Set aside.

- In a small saucepan, heat cream until hot but not boiling. Pour over chocolate morsels, and let sit until chocolate is melted, 1 to 2 minutes. Stir until chocolate is completely melted and creamy. Let chocolate ganache cool until slightly warm but not solidified.
- Place Chocolate Buttercream in a piping bag fitted with a medium round tip.
- Pipe buttercream onto tops of 16 cake layers, covering entire surface. Sprinkle each with ¼ teaspoon toffee bits. Top each with a second cake layer, and repeat with buttercream and toffee bits. Top each with a third cake layer, and spread with warm chocolate ganache. Sprinkle with remaining toffee bits.
- Garnish with fresh raspberries and sugared thyme, if desired.

For testing purposes, we used Hershey's Natural Unsweetened Cocoa.

†*For testing purposes, we used Ghirardelli 60% Cacao Bittersweet Chocolate Baking Chips.*

‡*For testing purposes, we used Heath Bits 'o Brickel Toffee Bits.*

**Spray fresh thyme with nonstick cooking spray, and sprinkle with superfine sugar.*

Chocolate Buttercream
Yield: 3 cups
Preparation: 5 minutes

1 cup salted butter, softened
3½ cups confectioners' sugar
6 tablespoons natural unsweetened cocoa powder
½ teaspoon salt
2 teaspoons vanilla extract
¼ cup whole milk

- In a large bowl, combine butter, confectioners' sugar, cocoa powder, salt, vanilla extract, and milk. Beat at low speed with an electric mixer until all ingredients are incorporated, scraping down sides of bowl as necessary. Increase speed to high, and beat until frosting is light and fluffy, 2 to 3 minutes.
- Store buttercream in the refrigerator for up to 1 day. Bring to room temperature before using.

Tea-Steeping GUIDE

The quality of the tea served at a tea party is as important as the food and the décor. To be sure your infusion is successful every time, here are some basic guidelines to follow.

WATER
Always use the best water possible. If the water tastes good, so will your tea. Heat the water on the stove top or in an electric kettle to the desired temperature. A microwave oven is not recommended.

TEMPERATURE
Heating the water to the correct temperature is arguably one of the most important factors in making a great pot of tea. Pouring boiling water on green, white, and oolong tea leaves can result in a very unpleasant brew. Always refer to the tea purveyor's packaging for specific instructions, but in general, use 170° to 195° water for these delicate tea types. Reserve boiling (212°) water for black and puerh teas, as well as herbal and fruit tisanes.

TEAPOT
If the teapot you plan to use is delicate, warm it with hot tap water first to avert possible cracking. Discard this water before adding the tea leaves or tea bags.

TEA
Use the highest-quality tea you can afford, whether loose leaf or prepackaged in bags or sachets. Remember that these better teas can often be steeped more than once. When using loose-leaf tea, generally use 1 teaspoon of dry leaf per 8 ounces of water, and use an infuser basket. For a stronger infusion, add another teaspoonful or two of dry tea leaf.

TIME
As soon as the water reaches the correct temperature for the type of tea, pour it over the leaves or tea bag in the teapot, and cover the pot with a lid. Set a timer—usually 1 to 2 minutes for whites and oolongs; 2 to 3 minutes for greens; and 3 to 5 minutes for blacks, puerhs, and herbals. (Steeping tea longer than recommended can yield a bitter infusion.) When the timer goes off, remove the infuser basket or the tea bags from the teapot.

ENJOYMENT
For best flavor, serve the tea as soon as possible. Keep the beverage warm atop a lighted warmer or under your favorite tea cozy if necessary.

How-tos

Let these step-by-step photos serve as your visual guide
while you create these impressive and delicious teatime
treats for your next party.

Coconut-Pecan Palmier Hearts, *page 26*

1. Fold in 2½ inches of opposite sides of dough square.

2. Repeat.

3. Fold half of dough over the other lengthwise.

4. Cut crosswise into 1-inch slices.

5. Dip cut sides of slices into sugar mixture.

6. Place cut side down on prepared baking sheet; pinch bottom fold.

Sweet Currant & Cranberry Tea Sandwiches, *page 25*

1. Using a 2¼-inch square cutter, cut squares from bread slices. Discard crusts.

2. Using a 1-inch heart-shaped cutter, remove centers from half of bread squares.

3. Spread cream-cheese mixture onto each bread square. Top with squares with centers removed.

Green Grape & Pistachio Cream Pavlovas, *page 36*

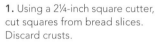

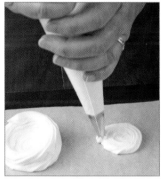

1. Line a baking sheet with parchment paper. Trace 2-inch circles onto parchment. Flip parchment over.

2. Starting in the middle of each traced circle, pipe concentric circles of meringue mixture outward until circle is filled.

3. Pipe 1 to 2 extra layers onto perimeters of rounds to form a rim around the edge of each circle.

4. Repeat piping procedure to fill all traced circles. Bake according to recipe.

5. Arrange grape halves in a circle in the pistachio cream in each baked meringue.

6. Arrange another circle of grape halves inside first circle to form a flower shape.

16 60 31 75

73 24 44 51

RECIPE INDEX

ACKNOWLEDGMENTS

New Year's Day
Recipe development and food styling by Loren Wood and Janet Lambert
Photography by Mac Jamieson and Sarah Swihart
Pages 8–19: Arte Italica *Bella Bianca* beaded dinner plate, salad plate, *Bella Bianca Flora* cup and saucer, and *Giglio* flatware 5-piece place setting, *arteitalica.com* for retailers. Juliska *Berry & Thread* 5-piece place setting in Ice Blue, *juliska.com. Charlie* linen place mats and napkins from Pom Pom at Home, 818-847-0150, *pompomathome.com*.
Page 9: Large *Bosphorus* bowls from Pottery Barn, 888-779-5176, *potterybarn.com*.
Page 11: *Incanto Lace* rectangular platter from Vietri, *vietri.com*.
Page 13: Sophie *Conran* white teapot from Amazon, *amazon.com*.
Page 16: Vietri *Incanto Lace* tray from Bromberg's at the Summit, 205-969-1776, *brombergs.com*.
Page 17: Arte Italica *Tuscan* medium oval platter, *arteitalica.com* for retailers.
Page 18: Simon Pearce *Hartland* Champagne flutes from Bromberg's in Mountain Brook, 205-871-3276, *brombergs.com*.

Valentine's Day
Recipe development and food styling by Loren Wood and Janet Lambert
Photography by Kamin H. Williams and Sarah Swihart
Pages 20–27: Floral arrangements by Flowerbuds, 205-970-3221, *flowerbudsinc.com*. Wedgwood *Ulander-Powder Ruby* 5-piece place setting and teapot, *wedgwoodusa.com*.
Page 25: Revol porcelain mini heart dish from Bed, Bath & Beyond, *bedbathandbeyond.com*.
Page 26: Juliska *Berry & Thread* rectangular serving tray from Bromberg's in Mountain Brook, 205-871-3276, *brombergs.com*.
Page 27: Julia Knight *Peony Heart* bowl from Bromberg's in Mountain Brook, 205-871-3276, *brombergs.com*.

St. Patrick's Day
Recipe development and food styling by Janet Lambert
Photography by William Dickey
Pages 28–37: Floral arrangements by Flowerbuds, 205-970-3221, *flowerbudsinc.com*. Lenox Kate Spade New York *Gardner Street Green* 5-piece place setting and oval platter, 800-223-4311, *lenox.com*. Royal Doulton *Precious Platinum* teapot from Replacements, 800-REPLACE, *replacements.com*. World Market Painterly Floral napkins, Fern Green buffet napkins, whitewash rattan square charger, and white buffet tablecloth, 877-967-5362, *worldmarket.com*.
Pages 30–31: Lenox Kate Spade New York *Gardner Street Green* serving bowl, 800-223-4311, *lenox.com*. Federal Glass Co. *Georgian Green* bowls and sherbert glasses from Replacements, 800-REPLACE, *replacements.com*.

Easter
Recipe development and food styling by Chantel Lambeth and Janet Lambert
Photography by Marcy Black Simpson and Sarah Swihart
Pages 38–47: Floral arrangements by Park Lane Flowers, 205-879-7115. Mottahedeh *Chelsea Botanicals* dinner plate, dessert plate, teacup, and saucer, *Imperatrice Blanc* teapot, and *Lace* service plate in Plum, 800-242-3050, *mottahedeh.com*. Moss runner from Davis Wholesale Florist, 205-595-2179. Julia Knight *Peony* rectangular tray from Bromberg's at the Summit, 205-969-1776, *brombergs.com*.
Page 43: Vietri *Incanto Curl* small platter from Bromberg's at the Summit, 205-969-1776, *brombergs.com*.

Mother's Day
Recipe development and food styling by Janet Lambert
Photography by Sarah Swihart and Marcy Black Simpson

Pages 48–57: Floral arrangements by Flowerbuds, 205-970-3221, *flowerbudsinc.com*. Herend charger in Lime, Herend *Royal Garden* dinner plate, salad plate, bread and butter plate, teacup, saucer, covered sugar bowl, creamer, and teapot, 800-643-7363, *herendusa.com*. Pom Pom at Home *Audrey* place mats and cotton napkins, *pompomathome.com* for retailers. Target brooches no longer available. Contact Target, 800-591-3869, *target.com*, for similar brooches.
Page 51: Waterford crystal bowl from Bromberg's in Mountain Brook, 205-871-3276, *brombergs.com*.
Page 52: Waterford crystal tiered stand from Bromberg's in Mountain Brook, 205-871-3276, *brombergs.com*.
Page 55: White ramekins from World Market, 877-967-5362, *worldmarket.com*.

Birthday
Recipe development and food styling by Janet Lambert
Photography by Sarah Swihart and Marcy Black Simpson
Pages 58–69: Floral arrangements by Flowerbuds, 205-970-3223, *flowerbudsinc.com*. Royal Crown Derby *Grenville* dinner plate, salad plate, cup and saucer, teapot, cream soup bowl, and oval platter from Replacements, 800-REPLACE, *replacements.com*. Pier 1 gold lacquer charger, 800-245-4595, *pier1.com*. Pottery Barn white linen hemstitch table runner, 888-779-5176, *potterybarn.com*. Garnier-Thiebaut napkins from Bromberg's in Mountain Brook, 205-871-3276, *brombergs.com*. Waterford *Lismore* 8-inch candlesticks and 4-inch candlesticks, 877-900-9973, *wwrd.com*.
Page 66: Crystal cake stand from a private collection.
Page 69: Tiered pedestal serving plates from Target, 800-591-3869, *target.com*.

Thanksgiving
Recipe development and food styling by Janet Lambert
Photography by Marcy Black Simpson
Pages 70–79: Floral arrangements by Michael's Fine Flowers, 205-949-1680. Mottahedeh *Sacred Bird & Butterfly* 5-piece place setting, 800-443-8225, *mottahedeh.com*. Casa Fina *Autumn Waves* dinner plate in pumpkin, *casafinagifts.com*. Pier 1 gold lacquer charger, 800-245-4595, *pier1.com*. Pier 1 table runner and napkins no longer available. Royal Doulton *Richelieu* teapot, creamer, and sugar from Replacements, 800-REPLACE, *replacements.com*.
Page 72: Small white pedestal, *rosannainc.com*.

Christmas
Recipe development and food styling by Janet Lambert
Photography by Mac Jamieson
Pages 80–90: Floral arrangements by Flowerbuds, 205-970-3223, *flowerbudsinc.com*. Royal Worcester *Holly Ribbons* cup and saucer, dinner plate, salad plate, and teapot; Mikasa *Parchment Red* chop plate from Replacements, 800-REPLACE, *replacements.com*. Pier 1 gold satin knot napkin, 800-245-4595, *pier1.com*. Towle *Old Master* Flatware 5-piece place setting from Macy's, *macys.com*.

....

SPECIALTY TEA PURVEYORS
The teas recommended in each of the menus are available from one or more of these fine companies.

Capital Teas, 888-484-8327, *capitalteas.com*
Harney & Sons, 888-427-6398, *harney.com*
Simpson & Vail, 800-282-8327, *svtea.com*
Tealuxe, 888-832-5893, *tealuxe.com*
Teas Etc, 800-832-1126, *teasetc.com*